Mometrix TEST PREPARATION

TerraNova® NEXT

Grade 4 Mathematics Test Prep Guide

Written and edited by the Mometrix Test Preparation Team
Printed in the United States of America

TABLE OF CONTENTS

Introduction

Thank you for purchasing this resource! You have made the choice to prepare yourself for a test that could have a huge impact on your future, and this guide is designed to help you be fully ready for test day. Obviously, it's important to have a solid understanding of the test material, but you also need to be prepared for the unique environment and stressors of the test, so that you can perform to the best of your abilities.

For this purpose, the first section that appears in this guide is the **Success Strategies**. We've devoted countless hours to meticulously researching what works and what doesn't, and we've boiled down our findings to the most impactful steps you can take to improve your performance on the test. We start at the beginning with study planning and move through the preparation process, all the way to the testing strategies that will help you get the most out of what you know when you're finally sitting in front of the test.

We recommend that you start preparing for your test as far in advance as possible. However, if you've bought this guide as a last-minute study resource and only have a few days before your test, we recommend that you skip over the first two Success Strategies since they address a long-term study plan.

If you struggle with **test anxiety**, we strongly encourage you to check out our recommendations for how you can overcome it. Test anxiety is a formidable foe, but it can be beaten, and we want to make sure you have the tools you need to defeat it.

Strategy #1 – Plan Big, Study Small

There's a lot riding on your performance. If you want to ace this test, you're going to need to keep your skills sharp and the material fresh in your mind. You need a plan that lets you review everything you need to know while still fitting in your schedule. We'll break this strategy down into three categories.

Information Organization

Start with the information you already have: the official test outline. From this, you can make a complete list of all the concepts you need to cover before the test. Organize these concepts into groups that can be studied together, and create a list of any related vocabulary you need to learn so you can brush up on any difficult terms. You'll want to keep this vocabulary list handy once you actually start studying since you may need to add to it along the way.

Time Management

Once you have your set of study concepts, decide how to spread them out over the time you have left before the test. Break your study plan into small, clear goals so you have a manageable task for each day and know exactly what you're doing. Then just focus on one small step at a time. When you manage your time this way, you don't need to spend hours at a time studying. Studying a small block of content for a short period each day helps you retain information better and avoid stressing over how much you have left to do. You can relax knowing that you have a plan to cover everything in time. In order for this strategy to be effective though, you have to start studying early and stick to your schedule. Avoid the exhaustion and futility that comes from last-minute cramming!

Study Environment

The environment you study in has a big impact on your learning. Studying in a coffee shop, while probably more enjoyable, is not likely to be as fruitful as studying in a quiet room. It's important to keep distractions to a minimum. You're only planning to study for a short block of time, so make the most of it. Don't pause to check your phone or get up to find a snack. It's also important to **avoid multitasking**. Research has consistently shown that multitasking will make your studying dramatically less effective. Your study area should also be comfortable and well-lit so you don't have the distraction of straining your eyes or sitting on an uncomfortable chair.

The time of day you study is also important. You want to be rested and alert. Don't wait until just before bedtime. Study when you'll be most likely to comprehend and remember. Even better, if you know what time of day your test will be, set that time aside for study. That way your brain will be used to working on that subject at that specific time and you'll have a better chance of recalling information.

Finally, it can be helpful to team up with others who are studying for the same test. Your actual studying should be done in as isolated an environment as possible, but the work of organizing the information and setting up the study plan can be divided up. In between study sessions, you can discuss with your teammates the concepts that you're all studying and quiz each other on the details. Just be sure that your teammates are as serious about the test as you are. If you find that your study time is being replaced with social time, you might need to find a new team.

Strategy #2 – Make Your Studying Count

You're devoting a lot of time and effort to preparing for this test, so you want to be absolutely certain it will pay off. This means doing more than just reading the content and hoping you can remember it on test day. It's important to make every minute of study count. There are two main areas you can focus on to make your studying count.

Retention

It doesn't matter how much time you study if you can't remember the material. You need to make sure you are retaining the concepts. To check your retention of the information you're learning, try recalling it at later times with minimal prompting. Try carrying around flashcards and glance at one or two from time to time or ask a friend who's also studying for the test to quiz you.

To enhance your retention, look for ways to put the information into practice so that you can apply it rather than simply recalling it. If you're using the information in practical ways, it will be much easier to remember. Similarly, it helps to solidify a concept in your mind if you're not only reading it to yourself but also explaining it to someone else. Ask a friend to let you teach them about a concept you're a little shaky on (or speak aloud to an imaginary audience if necessary). As you try to summarize, define, give examples, and answer your friend's questions, you'll understand the concepts better and they will stay with you longer. Finally, step back for a big picture view and ask yourself how each piece of information fits with the whole subject. When you link the different concepts together and see them working together as a whole, it's easier to remember the individual components.

Finally, practice showing your work on any multi-step problems, even if you're just studying. Writing out each step you take to solve a problem will help solidify the process in your mind, and you'll be more likely to remember it during the test.

Modality

Modality simply refers to the means or method by which you study. Choosing a study modality that fits your own individual learning style is crucial. No two people learn best in exactly the same way, so it's important to know your strengths and use them to your advantage.

For example, if you learn best by visualization, focus on visualizing a concept in your mind and draw an image or a diagram. Try color-coding your notes, illustrating them, or creating symbols that will trigger your mind to recall a learned concept. If you learn best by hearing or discussing information, find a study partner who learns the same way or read aloud to yourself. Think about how to put the information in your own words. Imagine that you are giving a lecture on the topic and record yourself so you can listen to it later.

For any learning style, flashcards can be helpful. Organize the information so you can take advantage of spare moments to review. Underline key words or phrases. Use different colors for different categories. Mnemonic devices (such as creating a short list in which every item starts with the same letter) can also help with retention. Find what works best for you and use it to store the information in your mind most effectively and easily.

Strategy #3 – Practice the Right Way

Your success on test day depends not only on how many hours you put into preparing, but also on whether you prepared the right way. It's good to check along the way to see if your studying is paying off. One of the most effective ways to do this is by taking practice tests to evaluate your progress. Practice tests are useful because they show exactly where you need to improve. Every time you take a practice test, pay special attention to these three groups of questions:

- The questions you got wrong
- The questions you had to guess on, even if you guessed right
- The questions you found difficult or slow to work through

This will show you exactly what your weak areas are, and where you need to devote more study time. Ask yourself why each of these questions gave you trouble. Was it because you didn't understand the material? Was it because you didn't remember the vocabulary? Do you need more repetitions on this type of question to build speed and confidence? Dig into those questions and figure out how you can strengthen your weak areas as you go back to review the material.

Additionally, many practice tests have a section explaining the answer choices. It can be tempting to read the explanation and think that you now have a good understanding of the concept. However, an explanation likely only covers part of the question's broader context. Even if the explanation makes perfect sense, **go back and investigate** every concept related to the question until you're positive you have a thorough understanding.

As you go along, keep in mind that the practice test is just that: practice. Memorizing these questions and answers will not be very helpful on the actual test because it is unlikely to have any of the same exact questions. If you only know the right answers to the sample questions, you won't be prepared for the real thing. **Study the concepts** until you understand them fully, and then you'll be able to answer any question that shows up on the test.

It's important to wait on the practice tests until you're ready. If you take a test on your first day of study, you may be overwhelmed by the amount of material covered and how much you need to learn. Work up to it gradually.

On test day, you'll need to be prepared for answering questions, managing your time, and using the test-taking strategies you've learned. It's a lot to balance, like a mental marathon that will have a big impact on your future. Like training for a marathon, you'll need to start slowly and work your way up. When test day arrives, you'll be ready.

Start with the strategies you've read in the first two Success Strategies—plan your course and study in the way that works best for you. If you have time, consider using multiple study resources to get different approaches to the same concepts. It can be helpful to see difficult concepts from more than one angle. Then find a good source for practice tests. Many times, the test website will suggest potential study resources or provide sample tests.

Practice Test Strategy

If you're able to find at least three practice tests, we recommend this strategy:

Untimed and Open-Book Practice

Take the first test with no time constraints and with your notes and study guide handy. Take your time and focus on applying the strategies you've learned.

Timed and Open-Book Practice

Take the second practice test open-book as well, but set a timer and practice pacing yourself to finish in time.

Timed and Closed-Book Practice

Take any other practice tests as if it were test day. Set a timer and put away your study materials. Sit at a table or desk in a quiet room, imagine yourself at the testing center, and answer questions as quickly and accurately as possible.

Keep repeating timed and closed-book tests on a regular basis until you run out of practice tests or it's time for the actual test. Your mind will be ready for the schedule and stress of test day, and you'll be able to focus on recalling the material you've learned.

Strategy #4 – Pace Yourself

Once you're fully prepared for the material on the test, your biggest challenge on test day will be managing your time. Just knowing that the clock is ticking can make you panic even if you have plenty of time left. Work on pacing yourself so you can build confidence against the time constraints of the exam. Pacing is a difficult skill to master, especially in a high-pressure environment, so **practice is vital**.

Set time expectations for your pace based on how much time is available. For example, if a section has 60 questions and the time limit is 30 minutes, you know you have to average 30 seconds or less per question in order to answer them all. Although 30 seconds is the hard limit, set 25 seconds per question as your goal, so you reserve extra time to spend on harder questions. When you budget extra time for the harder questions, you no longer have any reason to stress when those questions take longer to answer.

Don't let this time expectation distract you from working through the test at a calm, steady pace, but keep it in mind so you don't spend too much time on any one question. Recognize that taking extra time on one question you don't understand may keep you from answering two that you do understand later in the test. If your time limit for a question is up and you're still not sure of the answer, mark it and move on, and come back to it later if the time and the test format allow. If the testing format doesn't allow you to return to earlier questions, just make an educated guess; then put it out of your mind and move on.

On the easier questions, be careful not to rush. It may seem wise to hurry through them so you have more time for the challenging ones, but it's not worth missing one if you know the concept and just didn't take the time to read the question fully. Work efficiently but make sure you understand the question and have looked at all of the answer choices, since more than one may seem right at first.

Even if you're paying attention to the time, you may find yourself a little behind at some point. You should speed up to get back on track, but do so wisely. Don't panic; just take a few seconds less on each question until you're caught up. Don't guess without thinking, but do look through the answer choices and eliminate any you know are wrong. If you can get down to two choices, it is often worthwhile to guess from those. Once you've chosen an answer, move on and don't dwell on any that you skipped or had to hurry through. If a question was taking too long, chances are it was one of the harder ones, so you weren't as likely to get it right anyway.

On the other hand, if you find yourself getting ahead of schedule, it may be beneficial to slow down a little. The more quickly you work, the more likely you are to make a careless mistake that will affect your score. You've budgeted time for each question, so don't be afraid to spend that time. Practice an efficient but careful pace to get the most out of the time you have.

Test-Taking Strategies

This section contains a list of test-taking strategies that you may find helpful as you work through the test. By taking what you know and applying logical thought, you can maximize your chances of answering any question correctly!

It is very important to realize that every question is different and every person is different: no single strategy will work on every question, and no single strategy will work for every person. That's why we've included all of them here, so you can try them out and determine which ones work best for different types of questions and which ones work best for you.

Question Strategies

⊘ Read Carefully

Read the question and the answer choices carefully. Don't miss the question because you misread the terms. You have plenty of time to read each question thoroughly and make sure you understand what is being asked. Yet a happy medium must be attained, so don't waste too much time. You must read carefully and efficiently.

⊘ Contextual Clues

Look for contextual clues. If the question includes a word you are not familiar with, look at the immediate context for some indication of what the word might mean. Contextual clues can often give you all the information you need to decipher the meaning of an unfamiliar word. Even if you can't determine the meaning, you may be able to narrow down the possibilities enough to make a solid guess at the answer to the question.

⊘ Prefixes

If you're having trouble with a word in the question or answer choices, try dissecting it. Take advantage of every clue that the word might include. Prefixes can be a huge help. Usually, they allow you to determine a basic meaning. *Pre-* means before, *post-* means after, *pro-* is positive, *de-* is negative. From prefixes, you can get an idea of the general meaning of the word and try to put it into context.

⊘ Hedge Words

Watch out for critical hedge words, such as *likely, may, can, often, almost, mostly, usually, generally, rarely,* and *sometimes.* Question writers insert these hedge phrases to cover every possibility. Often an answer choice will be wrong simply because it leaves no room for exception. Be on guard for answer choices that have definitive words such as *exactly* and *always.*

⊘ Switchback Words

Stay alert for *switchbacks.* These are the words and phrases frequently used to alert you to shifts in thought. The most common switchback words are *but, although,* and *however.* Others include *nevertheless, on the other hand, even though, while, in spite of, despite,* and *regardless of*. Switchback words are important to catch because they can change the direction of the question or an answer choice.

⊘ Face Value

When in doubt, use common sense. Accept the situation in the problem at face value. Don't read too much into it. These problems will not require you to make wild assumptions. If you have to go beyond creativity and warp time or space in order to have an answer choice fit the question, then you should move on and consider the other answer choices. These are normal problems rooted in reality. The applicable relationship or explanation may not be readily apparent, but it is there for you to figure out. Use your common sense to interpret anything that isn't clear.

Answer Choice Strategies

⊘ Answer Selection

The most thorough way to pick an answer choice is to identify and eliminate wrong answers until only one is left, then confirm it is the correct answer. Sometimes an answer choice may immediately seem right, but be careful. The test writers will usually put more than one reasonable answer choice on each question, so take a second to read all of them and make sure that the other choices are not equally obvious. As long as you have time left, it is better to read every answer choice than to pick the first one that looks right without checking the others.

⊘ Answer Choice Families

An answer choice family consists of two (in rare cases, three) answer choices that are very similar in construction and cannot all be true at the same time. If you see two answer choices that are direct opposites or parallels, one of them is usually the correct answer. For instance, if one answer choice says that quantity *x* increases and another either says that quantity *x* decreases (opposite) or says that quantity *y* increases (parallel), then those answer choices would fall into the same family. An answer choice that doesn't match the construction of the answer choice family is more likely to be incorrect. Most questions will not have answer choice families, but when they do appear, you should be prepared to recognize them.

⊘ Eliminate Answers

Eliminate answer choices as soon as you realize they are wrong, but make sure you consider all possibilities. If you are eliminating answer choices and realize that the last one you are left with is also wrong, don't panic. Start over and consider each choice again. There may be something you missed the first time that you will realize on the second pass.

⊘ Avoid Fact Traps

Don't be distracted by an answer choice that is factually true but doesn't answer the question. You are looking for the choice that answers the question. Stay focused on what the question is asking for so you don't accidentally pick an answer that is true but incorrect. Always go back to the question and make sure the answer choice you've selected actually answers the question and is not merely a true statement.

⊘ Extreme Statements

In general, you should avoid answers that put forth extreme actions as standard practice or proclaim controversial ideas as established fact. An answer choice that states the "process should be used in certain situations, if…" is much more likely to be correct than one that states the "process should be discontinued completely." The first is a calm rational statement and doesn't even make a definitive, uncompromising stance, using a hedge word *if* to provide wiggle room, whereas the second choice is far more extreme.

⊘ Benchmark

As you read through the answer choices and you come across one that seems to answer the question well, mentally select that answer choice. This is not your final answer, but it's the one that will help you evaluate the other answer choices. The one that you selected is your benchmark or standard for judging each of the other answer choices. Every other answer choice must be compared to your benchmark. That choice is correct until proven otherwise by another answer choice beating it. If you find a better answer, then that one becomes your new benchmark. Once you've decided that no other choice answers the question as well as your benchmark, you have your final answer.

⊘ Predict the Answer

Before you even start looking at the answer choices, it is often best to try to predict the answer. When you come up with the answer on your own, it is easier to avoid distractions and traps because you will know exactly what to look for. The right answer choice is unlikely to be word-for-word what you came up with, but it should be a close match. Even if you are confident that you have the right answer, you should still take the time to read each option before moving on.

General Strategies

⊘ Tough Questions

If you are stumped on a problem or it appears too hard or too difficult, don't waste time. Move on! Remember though, if you can quickly check for obviously incorrect answer choices, your chances of guessing correctly are greatly improved. Before you completely give up, at least try to knock out a couple of possible answers. Eliminate what you can and then guess at the remaining answer choices before moving on.

⊘ Check Your Work

Since you will probably not know every term listed and the answer to every question, it is important that you get credit for the ones that you do know. Don't miss any questions through careless mistakes. If at all possible, try to take a second to look back over your answer selection and make sure you've selected the correct answer choice and haven't made a costly careless mistake (such as marking an answer choice that you didn't mean to mark). This quick double check should more than pay for itself in caught mistakes for the time it costs.

⊘ Pace Yourself

It's easy to be overwhelmed when you're looking at a page full of questions; your mind is confused and full of random thoughts, and the clock is ticking down faster than you would like. Calm down and maintain the pace that you have set for yourself. Especially as you get down to the last few minutes of the test, don't let the small numbers on the clock make you panic. As long as you are on track by monitoring your pace, you are guaranteed to have time for each question.

⊘ Don't Rush

It is very easy to make errors when you are in a hurry. Maintaining a fast pace in answering questions is pointless if it makes you miss questions that you would have gotten right otherwise. Test writers like to include distracting information and wrong answers that seem right. Taking a little extra time to avoid careless mistakes can make all the difference in your test score. Find a pace that allows you to be confident in the answers that you select.

⊘ Keep Moving

Panicking will not help you pass the test, so do your best to stay calm and keep moving. Taking deep breaths and going through the answer elimination steps you practiced can help to break through a stress barrier and keep your pace.

Final Notes

The combination of a solid foundation of content knowledge and the confidence that comes from practicing your plan for applying that knowledge is the key to maximizing your performance on test day. As your foundation of content knowledge is built up and strengthened, you'll find that the strategies included in this chapter become more and more effective in helping you quickly sift through the distractions and traps of the test to isolate the correct answer.

Now that you're preparing to move forward into the test content chapters of this book, be sure to keep your goal in mind. As you read, think about how you will be able to apply this information on the test. If you've already seen sample questions for the test and you have an idea of the question format and style, try to come up with questions of your own that you can answer based on what you're reading. This will give you valuable practice applying your knowledge in the same ways you can expect to on test day.

Good luck and good studying!

Operations and Algebraic Thinking

Representing Problems

Strip Diagrams

Strip diagrams can be used to solve addition, subtraction, multiplication, and division problems.

Addition and Subtraction

$$50 + a = 200$$

Set up a diagram.

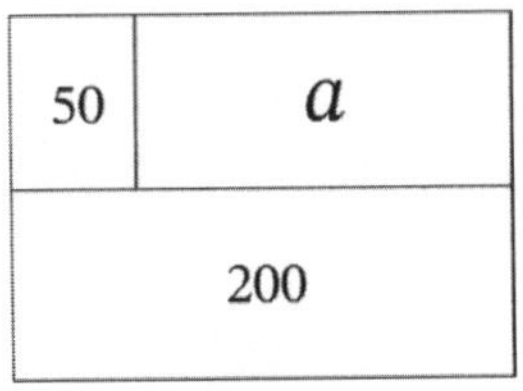

$$a = 150$$

$$28 - b = 16$$

Set up a diagram.

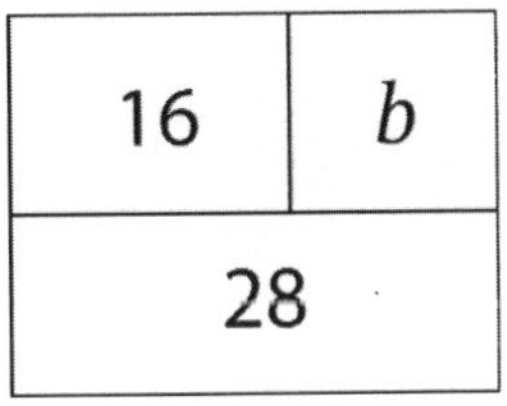

$$b = 12$$

Multiplication and Division

$$c \times 8 = 40$$

Set up a diagram.

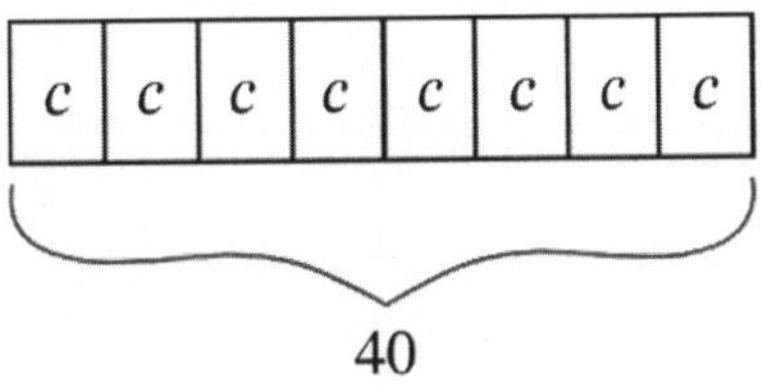

$$c = 5$$

$$25 \div d = 5$$

Set up a diagram.

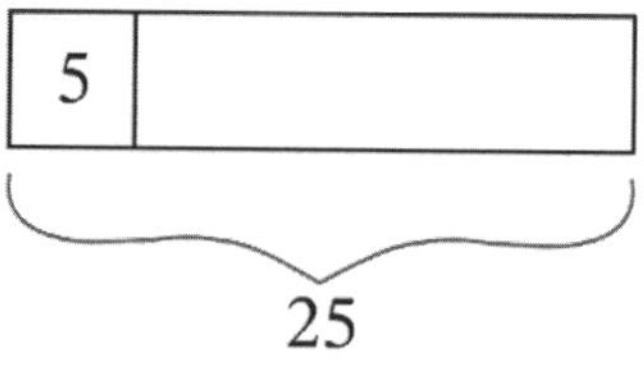

$$d = 5$$

Multi-Step Problems

$$100 - (45 \div 9)$$

Start by solving the section inside the parentheses.

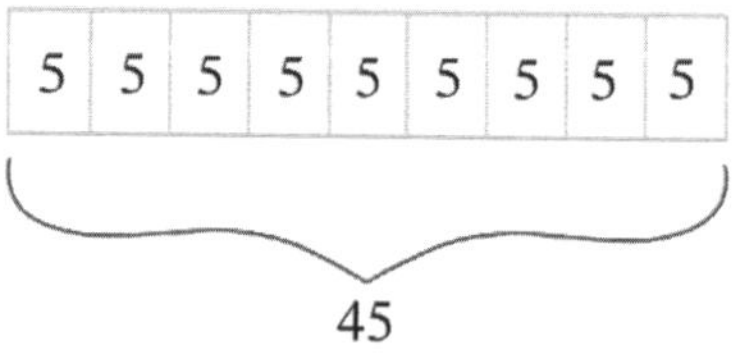

$$45 \div 9 = 5$$

Now subtract 5 from 100.

$$100 - 5 = 95$$

Example

Juniper Middle School has 330 students in 7th grade. There are a total of 11 classrooms, all with an equal number of students in each classroom. If each student needs 3 textbooks, how many textbooks are needed for the students in one classroom?

To figure out how many textbooks are needed for the students in one classroom, start by finding the number of students in each classroom. Since there are 330 total students and 11 classrooms, either of the following equations can be used to find the number of students in each classroom (s).

$$330 \div 11 = s$$

$$11 \times s = 330$$

In either case, $s = 30$, so there are 30 students in each classroom.

The next part of the question says that each student needs 3 textbooks, so to find the number of textbooks needed for all the students in one classroom, set up the following equation:

$$t = 3 \times 30$$

$$t = 90$$

This means that 90 textbooks are needed for the students in one classroom.

Example

Write two multiplication and division equations that can be represented by the tape diagram below.

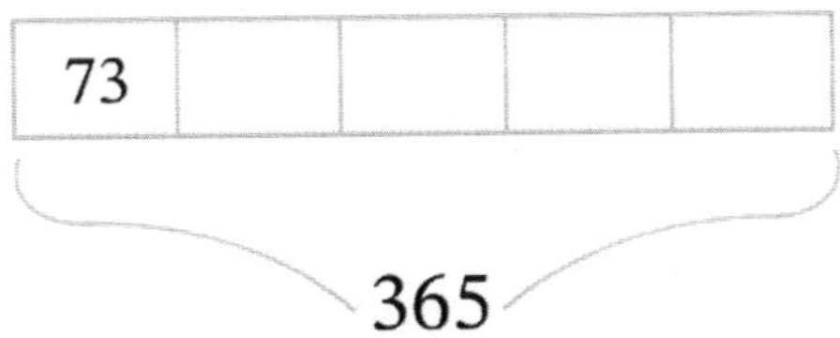

The tape diagram shows 5 equal sections of 73, with a total of 365. Two multiplication equations and two division equations can represent the model. Use fact families to create the following four equations:

$$365 \div 5 = 73$$
$$365 \div 73 = 5$$
$$5 \times 73 = 365$$
$$73 \times 5 = 365$$

Solving Multi-Step Word Problems

You and 7 friends are washing cars to earn money. The car wash costs \$5, and so far, 20 cars have been washed. If the earnings are split equally, how much money has each person earned so far?

Recall multiplication facts. Each car pays \$5, and 20 cars have been washed. $5 \times 2 = 10$, so $5 \times 20 = 100$. \$100 has been earned so far.

There are 8 friends in the group altogether. $100 \div 8$ can be solved using long division.

$$\begin{array}{r} 12\ R4 \\ 8\overline{)100} \\ \underline{-8} \\ 20 \\ \underline{-16} \\ 4 \end{array}$$

There is a remainder of 4. To express R4 in terms of money, start by writing the remainder as a fraction. R4 means $\frac{4}{8}$.

$$\frac{4}{8}$$

$$\begin{array}{r} 12 \text{ R}4 \\ 8\overline{)100} \\ -8 \\ \hline 20 \\ -16 \\ \hline 4 \end{array}$$

$\frac{4}{8}$ simplifies to $\frac{1}{2}$, which is the decimal 0.50. In terms of money, 0.50 is 50 cents. So, R4 represents 50 cents. Each person has earned \$12.50 so far.

Example

An artist sold 8 paintings at a craft fair. Each painting sold for \$16. The artist divided the earnings into 5 equal groups. How much money is in each group?

The scenario can be converted from word from to numeral form:

$$(16 \times 8) \div 5$$

Perform the operation in the parentheses first.

$$16 \times 8 = 128$$

Now divide 128 into 5 equal groups.

$$128 \div 5 = 25 \text{ r } 3$$

$$\begin{array}{r} 25\text{r}\,3 \\ 5\overline{)128} \\ -10 \\ \hline 28 \\ -25 \\ \hline 3 \end{array}$$

So,

$$128 \div 5 = 25 \text{ r } 3$$

In this case, remainder 3 means $\frac{3}{5}$ because the artist is dividing the money into 5 groups. $\frac{3}{5}$ is equivalent to $\frac{6}{10}$ or 0.6.

This means $128 \div 5 = 25.6$. The amount of money in each group is \$25.60.

Example

Mark has 3 boxes of cupcake mix. Each box makes 20 cupcakes. When Mark bakes the cupcakes, he can fit 10 cupcakes in each pan. If Mark uses the pan to make one batch of cupcakes at a time, how many times will he use the pan?

3 boxes that make 20 cupcakes each means 60 cupcakes: $3 \times 20 = 60$.

60 cupcakes are baked using 1 pan. Each pan holds 10 cupcakes, so divide 60 by 10: $60 \div 10 = 6$. This means the pan needs to be used 6 times.

Estimating Solutions

Problems involving addition, subtraction, multiplication, and division can be estimated before solving. Estimating before solving allows you to check an answer for **reasonableness**. For example, consider the problem $4{,}532 \div 8$. This can be estimated using compatible numbers. 4,532 is close to 4,500, and 8 is close to 9. These are considered **compatible numbers** because 4,500 can be quickly divided by 9.

$45 \div 9$ is 5.

$450 \div 9$ is 50.

$4{,}500 \div 9$ is 500.

This can be done using mental math, and this estimate can be compared to the "actual" answer. If the actual answer is close to 500, then the answer is likely correct.

$4{,}532 \div 8$ can be solved using long division:

```
        566  R4
    ___________
  8) 4,532
   - 4 0
     ---
      53
     -48
     ---
       52
      -48
      ---
        4
```

566 R4 is close to 500, so the answer is reasonable.

The reasonableness of an answer can be determined using estimation. For example, the product of 6,128 times 197 can be estimated quickly by rounding 6,128 to the nearest thousand, and rounding 197 to the nearest hundred.

6,128 becomes 6,000.

197 becomes 200.

$6{,}000 \times 200 = 1{,}200{,}000$

Remember, when rounding, first find the digit you are rounding, and then look to the digit to the right. If the digit to the right is 5 or more, the number rounds up. If the digit to the right is less than 5, the number stays the same.

For example, when rounding 6,284 to the nearest hundred, locate the digit in the hundreds place. 2 is in the hundreds place.

Now look to the right. The digit to the right of 2 is 8. 8 is 5 or more, so 2 will round up. 6,284 becomes 6,300. Notice how all digits to the right of the hundreds place become 0.

6,284

6,300

Patterns

A pattern is a particular arrangement of shapes, colors, pictures, numbers, objects, and other various things that repeats. Each pattern has a specific rule to follow. Patterns can also be referred to as sequences.

Example 1

Find the next number in each pattern:

1) 2, 4, 6, 8, ...

2) 5, 10, 15, 20, ...

3) 60, 50, 40, 30, ...

> 1) The numbers are increasing by 2. Add 2 to the last number to find the next number: 2, 4, 6, 8, 8 + 2 = 10.
>
> 2) The numbers are increasing by 5. Add 5 to the last number to find the next number: 5, 10, 15, 20, 20 + 5 = 25.
>
> 3) The numbers are decreasing by 10. Subtract 10 from the last number to find the next number: 60, 50, 40, 30, 30 – 10 = 20.

Example 2

Draw the next figure in this pattern:

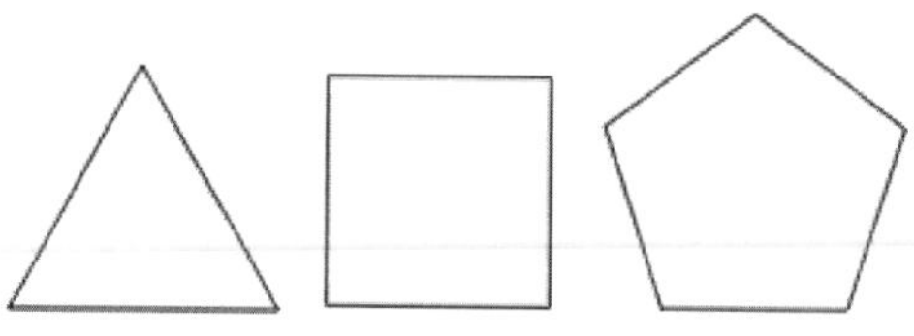

Look at the sides of each figure.

Figure 1: 3 sides

Figure 2: 4 sides

Figure 2: 5 sides

The number of sides on each figure is increasing by 1. The next figure will have 6 sides.

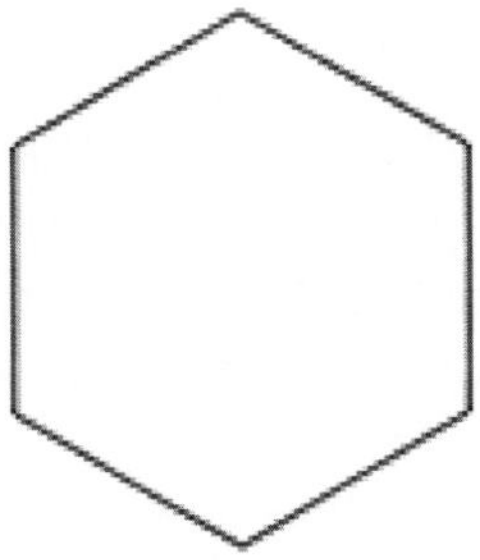

Example 3

Find the next figure in the pattern.

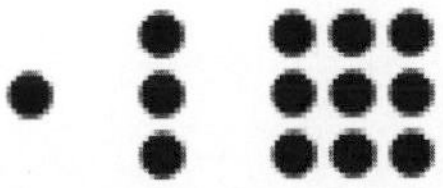

The first figure has 1 dot. The second has 3 dots. The third has 9 dots. Each figure is 3 times the size of the figure before it. The next figure will be three of the last figure:

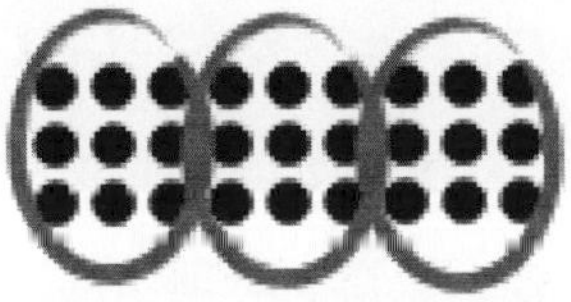

A figure that includes three of the last figure has $3 \cdot 9 = 27$ dots.

Recalling Multiplication Facts

It is a great accomplishment to memorize the multiplication and division facts from 0 to 10. This is a goal that can take some time, so keep practicing!

Some strategies that can help:

1. **Skip count by the larger number.** For example, for the problem 8×3 skip count by 8s not 3s. This can save some time. $8 + 8 + 8$ is quicker than $3 + 3 + 3 + 3 + 3 + 3 + 3 + 3$.
2. **Use facts that you do know to help you.** For example, if you are stuck on 7×4 but you know 5×7 is 35, use logic to help you. 5 groups of 7 is 7 more than 4 groups of 7, so subtract 7 from 35 to solve 4×7.

3. **Use multiplication to help with division.** Multiplication and division are inverse operations. This means they undo each other. For example, $9 \times 4 = 36$ and $4 \times 9 = 36$ represent the inverse of $36 \div 4 = 9$ and $36 \div 9 = 4$. Your multiplication facts and division facts go hand-in-hand! Remember, multiplication and division fact families use the same three numbers. For example, $8 \times 7 = 56$, $7 \times 8 = 56$, $56 \div 7 = 8$, and $56 \div 8 = 7$ all use the same three numbers.

Finding Unknown Numbers

Inverse Operations

Multiplication and division go hand in hand. Division and multiplication are considered **inverse operations**, which means they are the reverse, or opposite, of each other. This can be helpful when there is an **unknown number** in an equation. For example, $4 \times ? = 24$ is a multiplication equation that can be solved using division. $24 \div 4 = 6$, therefore $4 \times 6 = 24$. The missing number is 6.

Let's try another example: $72 \div ? = 9$. This is a division equation that can be solved using multiplication. What number times 9 equals 72? The missing number is 8.

Fact Families

Don't forget to use **fact families** when solving equations with **missing numbers**.

For example, the equations $5 \times 8 = 40$, $8 \times 5 = 40$, $40 \div 5 = 8$, $40 \div 8 = 5$ represent a fact family. The same three numbers are used in all the equations. This can be helpful when one of the numbers is missing. For example, $8 \times ? = 40$. Remember the fact families. 8 groups of 5 equals 40, so the missing number is 5.

$$\text{Factor} \times \text{Factor} = \text{Product}$$

$$8 \times 5 = 40$$

8 and 5 are considered factors, and 40 is the product.

Factors and Multiples

Factors and Greatest Common Factor

Factors are numbers that are multiplied together to obtain a **product**. For example, in the equation $2 \times 3 = 6$, the numbers 2 and 3 are factors. A **prime number** has only two factors (1 and itself), but other numbers can have many factors.

A **common factor** is a number that divides exactly into two or more other numbers. For example, the factors of 12 are 1, 2, 3, 4, 6, and 12, while the factors of 15 are 1, 3, 5, and 15. The common factors of 12 and 15 are 1 and 3.

A **prime factor** is also a prime number. Therefore, the prime factors of 12 are 2 and 3. For 15, the prime factors are 3 and 5.

The **greatest common factor** (**GCF**) is the largest number that is a factor of two or more numbers. For example, the factors of 15 are 1, 3, 5, and 15; the factors of 35 are 1, 5, 7, and 35. Therefore, the greatest common factor of 15 and 35 is 5.

Review Video: Factors
Visit mometrix.com/academy and enter code: 920086

Review Video: Prime Numbers and Factorization
Visit mometrix.com/academy and enter code: 760669

Review Video: Greatest Common Factor and Least Common Multiple
Visit mometrix.com/academy and enter code: 838699

Multiples and Least Common Multiple

Often listed out in multiplication tables, **multiples** are integer increments of a given factor. In other words, dividing a multiple by the factor will result in an integer. For example, the multiples of 7 include: $1 \times 7 = 7, 2 \times 7 = 14, 3 \times 7 = 21, 4 \times 7 = 28, 5 \times 7 = 35$. Dividing 7, 14, 21, 28, or 35 by 7 will result in the integers 1, 2, 3, 4, and 5, respectively.

The least common multiple (**LCM**) is the smallest number that is a multiple of two or more numbers. For example, the multiples of 3 include 3, 6, 9, 12, 15, etc.; the multiples of 5 include 5, 10, 15, 20, etc. Therefore, the least common multiple of 3 and 5 is 15.

Review Video: Multiples
Visit mometrix.com/academy and enter code: 626738

Numbers and Operations in Base Ten

Base-Ten Number System

In the **base ten number system**, digits **increase** by a **factor of 10** as you move to the **left** and **decrease** by a factor of 10 as you move to the **right**. For example, 55.55 shows 5 in the hundredths place, 5 in the tenths place, 5 in the ones place, and 5 in the tens place. Digits are 10 times as large as you move to the left. As you move to the right, the digits are one-tenth the previous digit. Consider the following example.

$$45 \times 10 = 450$$

$$45 \times 100 = 4{,}500$$

$$45 \times 1{,}000 = 45{,}000$$

$$45 \times 10{,}000 = 450{,}000$$

The important thing to remember is that each place value increases by a factor of 10. Another way to think about this is $45 \times 10 \times 10 \times 10 \times 10 = 450{,}000$.

This also applies to fraction and decimal values. Consider the following examples.

Moving to the left:

$\frac{5}{10}$ is 10 times as large as $\frac{5}{100}$.

5 is 10 times as large as $\frac{5}{10}$.

50 is 10 times as large as 5.

Moving to the right:

5 is $\frac{1}{10}$ of 50.

0.5 is $\frac{1}{10}$ of 5.

0.05 is $\frac{1}{10}$ of 0.5.

Review Video: Number Place Value
Visit mometrix.com/academy and enter code: 205433

Expanded Notation

Expanded notation shows the value of each digit in a number. For example, 45.3 can be "expanded" into 4 tens, 5 ones, and 3 tenths. In expanded form, it is $40 + 5 + 0.3$.

The following number is in **standard form**: 1,234,567,891.23

When writing numbers in expanded form, consider the place value of each number.

The first 1 represents 1,000,000,000.
The first 2 represents 200,000,000.
The first 3 represents 30,000,000.
The 4 represents 4,000,000.
The 5 represents 500,000.
The 6 represents 60,000.
The 7 represents 7,000.
The 8 represents 800.
The 9 represents 90.
The second 1 represents 1.
The second 2 represents 0.2.
The second 3 represents 0.03.

Put it all together in expanded form:

$$1{,}000{,}000{,}000 + 200{,}000{,}000 + 30{,}000{,}000 + 4{,}000{,}000 + 500{,}000 + 60{,}000 + 7{,}000 + 800 + 90 + 1 + 0.2 + 0.03$$

Review Video: Place Value
Visit mometrix.com/academy and enter code: 205433

Example

Write the number 567.92 in expanded form.

Standard form: 567.92

Expanded form: $500 + 60 + 7 + 0.9 + 0.02$

Example

What is the value of the first 5 in the number 45,105,000?

The first 5 is in the millions place , so its value is 5,000,000.

Whole Numbers

Comparing Whole Numbers

When comparing whole numbers, compare each digit from left to right. For example, consider the comparison between the numbers 46,241,733 and 46,243,946. At first glance, the numbers might seem very close. To precisely compare the numbers, compare each digit, one by one, starting at the **farthest left digit**.

46 , 241 , 733

46 , 243 , 946

Both digits have 4 in the ten millions place.

Both digits have 6 in the millions place.

Both digits have 2 in the hundred thousands place.

Both digits have 4 in the ten thousands place.

The top number has 1 in the thousands place, but the bottom number has 3 in the thousands place. 3 > 1 so 46,243,946 > 46,241,733.

Symbols for Comparing Numbers

Remember that the symbol > means "is **greater** than." When using this symbol, the larger number must appear first, or to the left of the symbol. The symbol < means "is **less** than." So when using this symbol, the smaller number must appear first, or to the left of the symbol. When using the symbol =, the equal sign, the numbers on both sides of the symbol should have the **same** value.

Rounding Whole Numbers

When rounding whole numbers, look at the number to the **right** of the digit you are **rounding**. If the number to the right is **5 or more**, the digit you are rounding rounds **up**. If the number to the right is **less than 5**, the digit you are rounding stays the **same**. All the digits to the right of the one you are rounding become **zeros**.

Round to the nearest ten: 392,537

Find the digit in the tens place (3). Look to the right. 7 is "5 or more", so the digit 3 will round up to 4. All digits to the right of 4 become 0.

392,537 becomes 392,540.

Round to the nearest hundred: 392,537.

Find the digit in the hundreds place (5). Look to the right. 3 is "less than 5", so the digit 5 will stay the same. All digits to the right of 5 become 0.

392,537 becomes 392,500.

Round to the nearest thousand: 392,537. Find the digit in the thousands place (2). Look to the right. 5 is "5 or more", so the digit 2 will round up to 3. All digits to the right of the rounded 3 become 0.

392,537 becomes 393,000.

Addition and Subtraction Problems

Some word problems can be solved in one step. For example, suppose a baker makes 35 cakes and 150 cookies each day. Altogether, how many treats are baked each day? This can be solved in one step, using one operation. $35 + 150 = 185$. 185 treats are baked each day.

More advanced word problems will require two steps. For example, suppose a painter earns $450 for every room that they paint. After 2 rooms are completed, the painter spends $185 on more paint supplies. How much money remains? Many two-step problems can be solved using strategies such as drawing a picture or model, using a number line, or solving an equation.

Pictures and Models

Use base ten blocks to represent 185 taken from 2 groups of 450 to get 715.

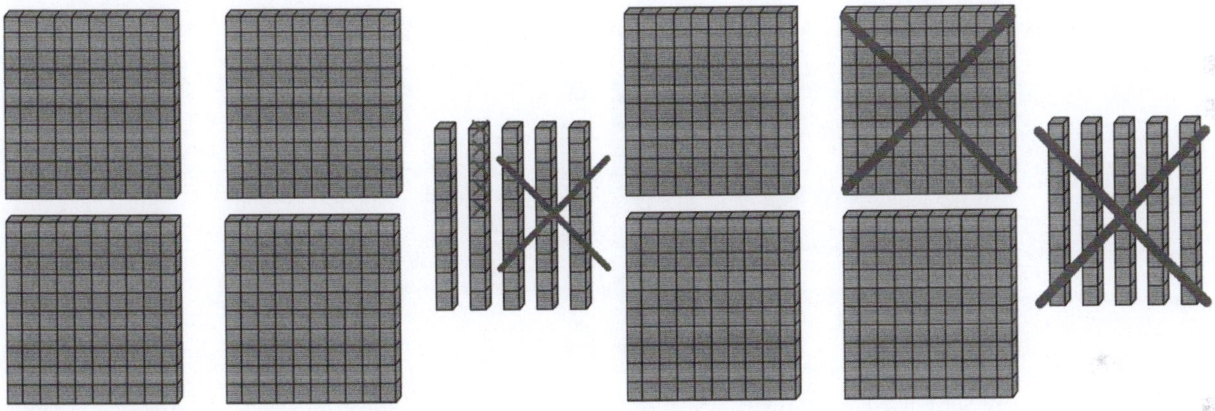

Number Lines

Make two jumps of 450, then back 185.

$$(450 + 450) - 185 = 715$$

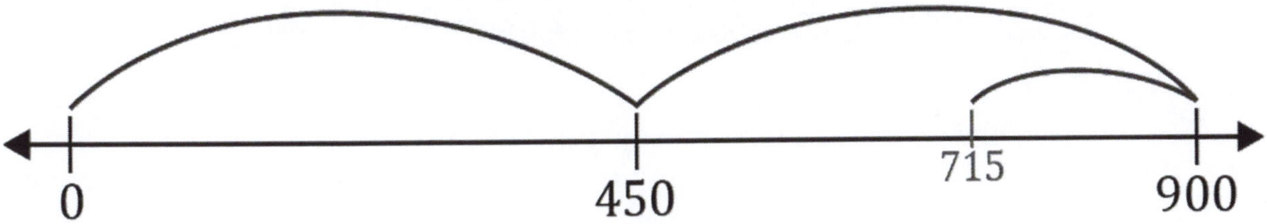

Equations

$$m = (450 + 450) - 185$$

The equation simplifies to $m = 715$, or $715.

Example

Use the number line to represent $200 + 50 - 125$.

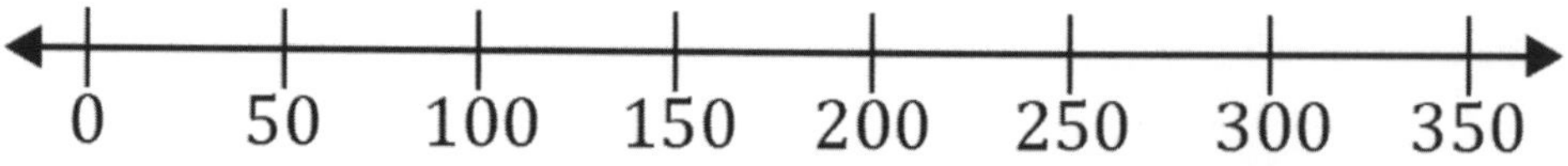

Start by adding 50 to 200. Make one jump forward from 200 to 250.

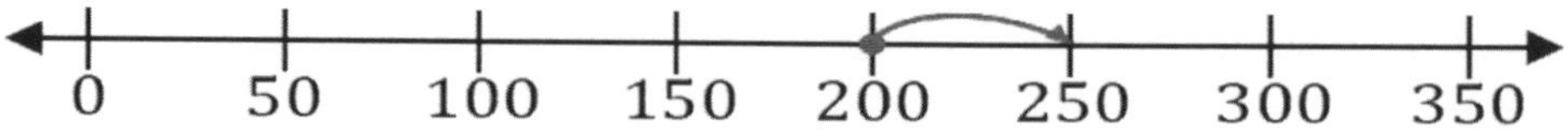

Now subtract 125. Jump back 100 and then back 25 more. 250 becomes 150 and then 125.

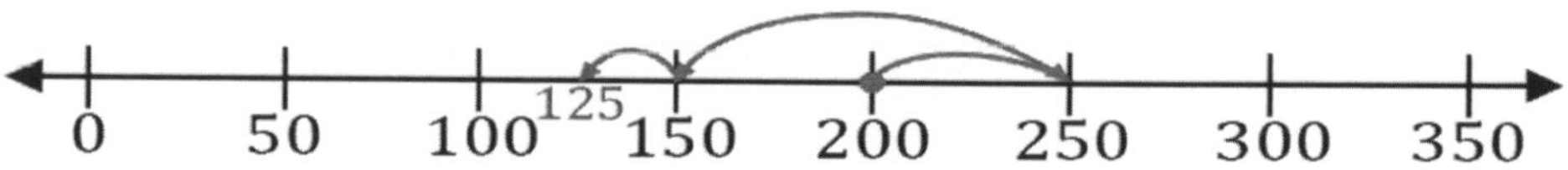

$$200 + 50 - 125 = 125.$$

EXAMPLE

Write and solve a subtraction equation that matches the model below.

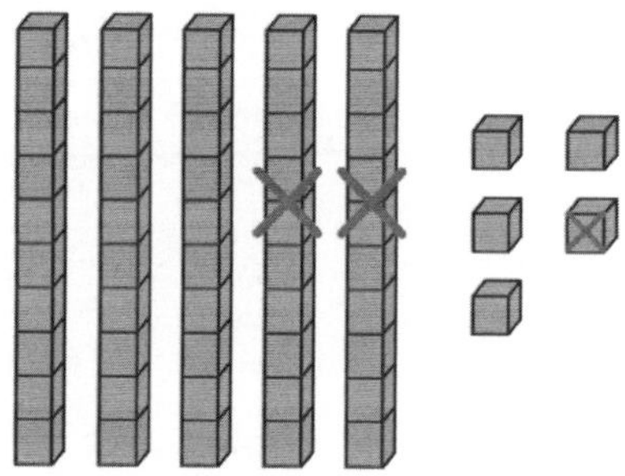

The model shows 5 groups of ten plus 5 groups of one, which represents 55. Then 2 groups of ten and 1 group of one are crossed out. This represents subtraction of 21. This leaves 3 groups of ten and 4 groups of one. So, 55 − 21 leaves 34 remaining. The answer is $55 - 21 = 34$.

> **Review Video: Adding Large Numbers**
> Visit mometrix.com/academy and enter code: 347073

PLACE VALUE STRATEGY

One- and two-step **addition and subtraction problems** can be solved using place value. For example, 432 + 826 can be thought of as a group of 4 hundreds, 3 tens, and 2 ones, plus 8 hundreds, 2 tens, and 6 ones. Combine the place values to solve:

$$4 \text{ hundreds} + 8 \text{ hundreds} = 12 \text{ hundreds}$$

$$3 \text{ tens} + 2 \text{ tens} = 5 \text{ tens}$$

$$2 \text{ ones} + 6 \text{ ones} = 8 \text{ ones}$$

$$1{,}200 + 50 + 8 = 1{,}258$$

STANDARD ALGORITHM

A small backyard swimming pool contains 3,398 gallons of water. A pool cleaning company is draining the pool to clean the interior of the pool. At noon the pool contains 2,129 gallons of water. How many gallons of water has been drained from the pool so far?

1,269 gallons

The pool started with 3,398 gallons of water and at noon contains 2,129 gallons. Subtract to determine the number of gallons that have been drained. Use the standard algorithm, and stack 3,398 over 2,129 so that the place value is lined up. Subtract columns from right to left. Regroup if necessary: $3,398 - 2,129 = 1,269$.

$$\begin{array}{r} 1 \\ 88 \\ 33\cancel{9}\cancel{8} \\ -2129 \\ \hline 1269 \end{array}$$

The pool has drained 1,269 gallons of water by noon.

Two-Step Addition and Subtraction Problems

Consider the scenario: A shopper starts with $456 in their wallet and then spends $128 on shoes. Later that day, the shopper finds a 20-dollar bill in their pocket. Altogether, how much money does the shopper have left after shoe shopping?

The scenario can be solved in two steps. The shopper starts with $456 and then spends $128. This means that $128 have been subtracted from $456. $456 consists of 4 hundreds, 5 tens, and 6 ones. $128 consists of 1 hundred, 2 tens, and 8 ones. 8 ones cannot be subtracted from 6 ones, which means **regrouping** needs to occur.

4 hundreds, 5 tens, and 6 ones becomes 4 hundreds, 4 tens, and 16 ones. Now subtraction can continue: $456 - 128 = 328$.

$$\begin{array}{r} 4\ 5\ 6 \\ -\ 1\ 2\ 8 \\ \hline \end{array} \rightarrow \begin{array}{r} {\scriptstyle 4\ 16} \\ 4\ \cancel{5}\ \cancel{6} \\ -\ 1\ 2\ 8 \\ \hline 3\ 2\ 8 \end{array}$$

The shopper then finds $20 in their pocket. This indicates adding 20: $328 + 20 = 348$.

The shopper has $348 after shoe shopping.

EXAMPLE

Find the value of the expression below:

$$(648 + 250) - 30$$

648 consists of 6 hundreds, 4 tens, and 8 ones. 250 consists of 2 hundreds, 5 tens, and 0 ones. Combine each place value to find the sum.

$$600 + 200 + 40 + 50 + 8 + 0 = 898$$

Now, subtract 30, which consists of 3 tens, from 898. 898 consists of 9 tens. Subtract 3 tens from this: $898 - 30 = 868$.

$$(648 + 250) - 30 = 868$$

The answer is 868.

EXAMPLE

Find the value of the expression below:

$$640 - 180$$

Think about 640 and 180 in terms of place value.

$$640 = 6 \text{ hundreds} + 4 \text{ tens} + 0 \text{ ones}$$

$$180 = 1 \text{ hundred} + 8 \text{ tens} + 0 \text{ ones}$$

640 has 4 tens, which is not enough to subtract 8 tens from.

Regrouping is necessary. 1 of the hundreds becomes 10 tens. So, 6 hundreds + 4 tens + 0 ones becomes 5 hundreds + 14 tens + 0 ones.

Now subtraction can begin.

(5 hundreds + 14 tens + 0 ones) − (1 hundred + 8 tens + 0 ones) becomes

4 hundreds + 6 tens + 0 ones. In standard form, this is 460.

$$640 - 180 = 460$$

The answer is 460.

Multiplying by 10 and 100

When multiplying by 10, the decimal point moves **one place** to the **right**. When multiplying by 100, the decimal point moves **two places** to the **right**. The pattern continues for each multiple of 10. This is a convenient way to multiply numbers by powers of 10. For example, notice the decimal movement in the following examples:

$$45.62 \times 10 = 456.2$$

$$45.62 \times 100 = 4{,}562.0$$

The same pattern can be seen when multiplying whole numbers. Any whole number can be expressed as a decimal. Think about where the decimal point is in the number 50.

Sometimes the decimal point is not written for whole numbers, but it's technically there. 50 has a "decimal" to the right of the ones place. Remember, a decimal separates the ones place from the tenths place. 50 is equal to 50.0.

$$50.0 \times 10 = 500.0$$

Notice how the decimal moves one place to the right.

$$50.0 \times 100 = 5{,}000.0$$

Notice how the decimal moves two places to the right.

Multiplication with Multiple-Digit Numbers

Area Models

There are a variety of strategies to choose from when multiplying multi-digit numbers. Area models and arrays can be used to show multiplication in a visual way, as opposed to the standard algorithm. For example, consider the problem 8×11. This can be represented as an **array** with 8 columns and 11 rows. There are 8 groups of 11 stars, or 11 groups of 8 stars. The total number of stars is 88, so $8 \times 11 = 88$. This strategy is great for smaller numbers. However, when multiplying two-digit numbers an area model is often preferred.

An **area model** is a visual representation of the distributive property. For example, when multiplying 27 by 35, the distributive property would be expressed as $7 \times 5 + 7 \times 30 + 20 \times 5 + 20 \times 30$. An area model shows this process using boxes. Set up each two-digit number as shown. Break apart 27 into 20 and 7. Break apart 35 into 30 and 5. Fill in each box by multiplying the outside numbers. $30 \times 20 = 600$, $30 \times 7 = 210$, $5 \times 20 = 100$, $5 \times 7 = 35$, and the sum of all the products is $600 + 100 + 210 + 35 = 945$. Therefore, $27 \times 35 = 945$.

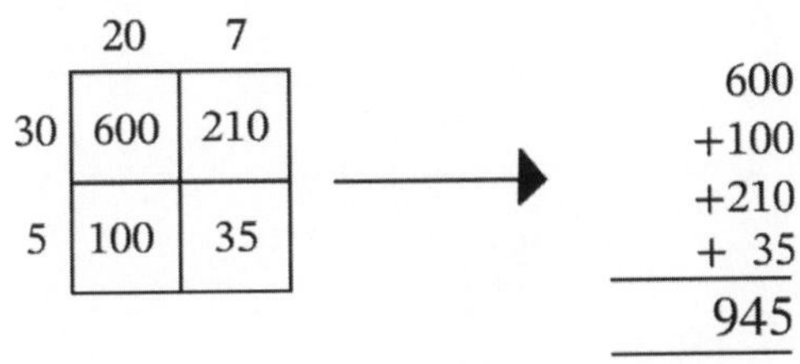

$$27 \times 35 = 945$$

Standard Algorithm

Area models and arrays are great strategies for one and two-digit multiplication. However, the **standard algorithm** is a commonly preferred strategy for numbers that are more than three digits. The standard algorithm, or "vertical multiplication" is less visual but more time effective. For example, consider the product 7,482 × 8. Write the longer number on the top and the shorter number on the bottom. Push all numbers to the right so that the place value is lined up (ones lined up with ones, tens lined up with tens, etc.).

$$\begin{array}{r} {\scriptstyle 3\ \ 6\,1\ } \\ 7{,}482 \\ \times \qquad 8 \\ \hline 59{,}856 \end{array}$$

Distribute, or multiply, the 8 by each digit in the number 7,482. Work from right to left. 8 × 2, then 8 × 8, then 8 × 4, then 8 × 7. If a product has more than one digit, write the ones digit in the answer and carry the tens digit above the next number you are multiplying. For example, 2 × 8 = 16, so write 6 in the answer and 1 above 8 (the next number you will multiply by). Then, add the carried number to the next product. 8 × 8 = 64, then add 1 to get 65, and continue the multiplication process for the rest of the number. The product of 7,482 and 8 is 59,856.

Partial Products

Using partial products is another option when multiplying multi-digit numbers. For example, consider the problem 48 × 26.

Using **partial products** is one way to express the distributive property. In the problem 48 × 26, each digit needs to be multiplied by every other digit, according to its place value. Using partial products breaks this down into pieces.

$$\begin{array}{c} 6 \times 8 = 48 \\ 6 \times 40 = 240 \\ 20 \times 8 = 160 \\ 20 \times 40 = 800 \end{array}$$

$$\begin{array}{r} 48 \\ \times 26 \\ \hline 48 \\ 240 \\ 160 \\ +800 \\ \hline 1\,248 \end{array}$$

The sum of these "partial products" is 1,248.

Division with Multiple-Digit Numbers

Area Models

Long division is not the only way to divide multi-digit numbers. You can also use an **area model**. 620 ÷ 5 can be solved by drawing a rectangle with 5 as one side length. Now think in terms of multiplication. 5 × 100 is close to 620. Start with this. Write 100 above the rectangle. 5 × 100 = 500. So, write 500 in the first box.

620 − 500 = 120, so now think about multiplying 5 by a number to get close to 120. 5 × 20 is 100, so start there. Write 20 above the rectangle. Since 5 × 20 = 100, write 100 in the next box.

120 − 100 = 20, so now think about multiplying 5 by a number to get close to 20. 5 × 4 is 20, so write 4 above the rectangle. Write 20 in the last box.

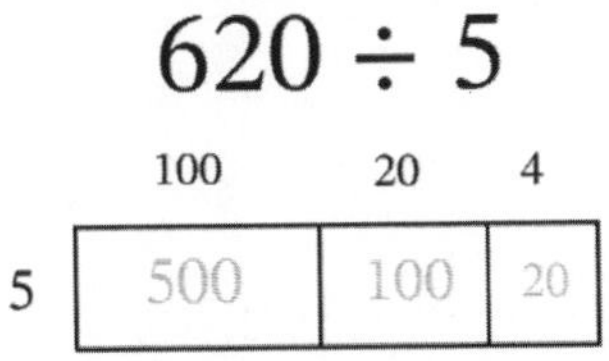

Now add up the numbers above the rectangle. 100 + 20 + 4 = 124, therefore 620 ÷ 5 = 124.

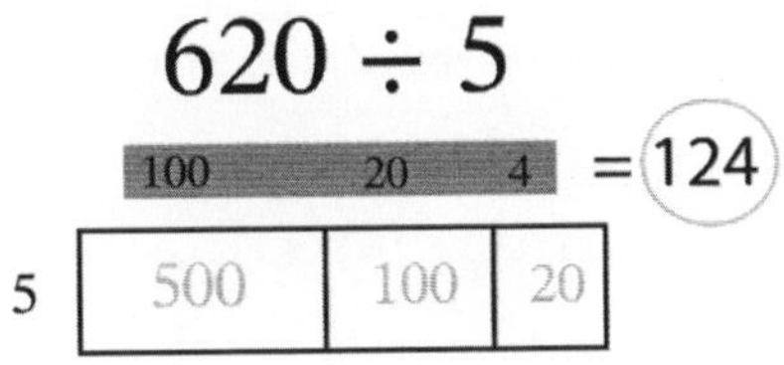

Long Division

The **standard algorithm** for division, also known as **long division**, is a great option for division problems involving large numbers. The long division process involves 4 steps that repeat in a cycle.

The divisor goes to the left of the division sign, and the dividend goes under the division sign. For example, in the problem 6,488 ÷ 2, the divisor is 2 and the dividend is 6,488.

$$2\overline{)6,488}$$

The four steps of long division:

1. "How many times?"
2. Multiply
3. Subtract
4. Bring down

EXAMPLE

1. 2 fits into 6, 3 times. Write 3.
2. $3 \times 2 = 6$. Write 6.
3. Subtract. $6 - 6 = 0$.
4. Bring down the next digit, which is 4.

```
    3
2)6,488
 -6↓
  0 4
```

Repeat this 4-step process until there are no more digits to "bring down". The result is $6{,}488 \div 2 = 3{,}244$.

```
   3,244
2)6,488
 -6
  0 4
  - 4
    08
    -8
     08
     -8
      0
```

Numbers and Operations – Fractions

Decimals

Representing Decimals with Models

It can be helpful to **visualize** fractions and decimals as a **model**. For example, when one whole is divided into 10 equal shares, each share represents 1 out of 10. As a fraction this is $\frac{1}{10}$, and as a decimal this is 0.1.

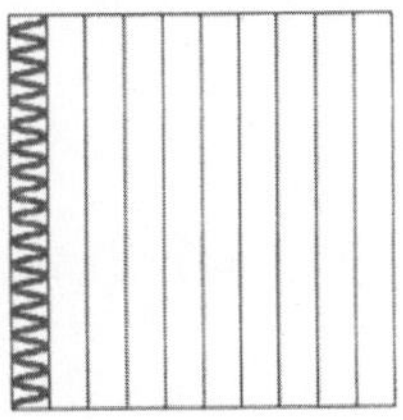

When one whole is divided into 100 equal shares, each share represents 1 out of 100. As a fraction this is $\frac{1}{100}$, and as a decimal this is 0.01.

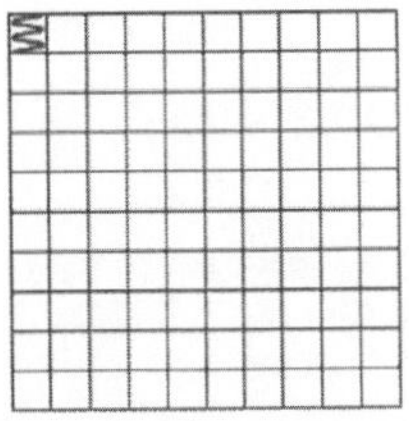

Notice how 1 out of 10 is the same amount as 10 out of 100. So, $\frac{1}{10}$ and $\frac{10}{100}$ are considered equivalent fractions. This means 0.1 and 0.10 are considered equivalent decimals.

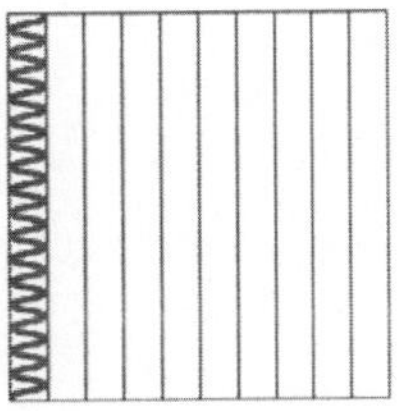

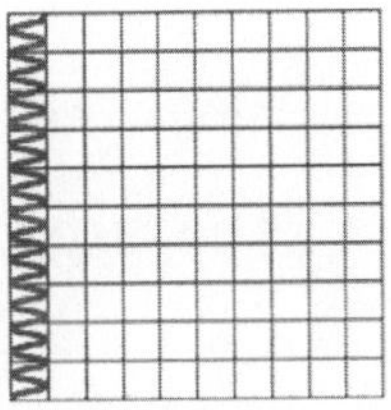

REPRESENTING DECIMALS WITH MONEY

Money is expressed in **dollars** and **cents**. Cents are represented as **tenths** and **hundredths**. For example, \$4.92 represents 4 whole dollars, 9 tenths of a dollar, and 2 hundredths of a dollar.

Express the coins as a decimal dollar amount:

4 quarters, 4 nickels, 2 pennies.

4 quarters: $\$0.25 + \$0.25 + \$0.25 + \$0.25 = \$1.00$

4 nickels: $\$0.05 + \$0.05 + \$0.05 + \$0.05 = \$0.20$

2 pennies: $\$0.01 + \$0.01 = \$0.02$

Remember, line up the decimal points when adding decimals.

$$\begin{array}{r} 1.\ 00 \\ 0.\ 20 \\ +0.\ 02 \\ \hline \$1.\ 22 \end{array}$$

EXAMPLE

Consider the model below. What fraction would this represent? What decimal? What dollar amount?

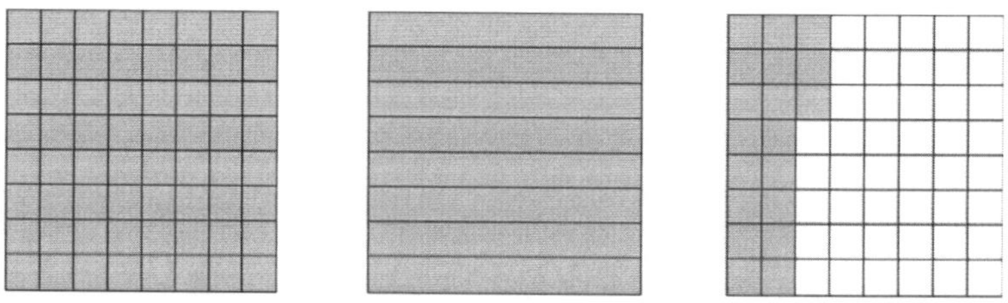

The model shows $\frac{100}{100} + \frac{10}{10} + \frac{23}{100}$.

This represents 2 wholes and 23 hundredths.

As a decimal, this is 2.23.

As a dollar amount, this represents \$2.23.

COMPARING AND ORDERING DECIMALS

Decimals can be compared and ordered by **comparing each digit** from left to right. For example, 13.84 and 13.54 have the same digit in the tens place (1), the same digit in the ones place (3), but they have a different digit in the tenths place. Comparing these values, we see $8 > 5$, which means 13.84 is greater than 13.54.

This can also be seen using a visual model. For example, when comparing decimals in a model, the larger decimal value will cover a larger portion of the whole. The model on the left shows 6 out of 10, or 0.6. The model on the right shows 13 out of 100, or 0.13. Notice how 0.6 has a larger shaded region. This means 0.6 is greater than 0.13.

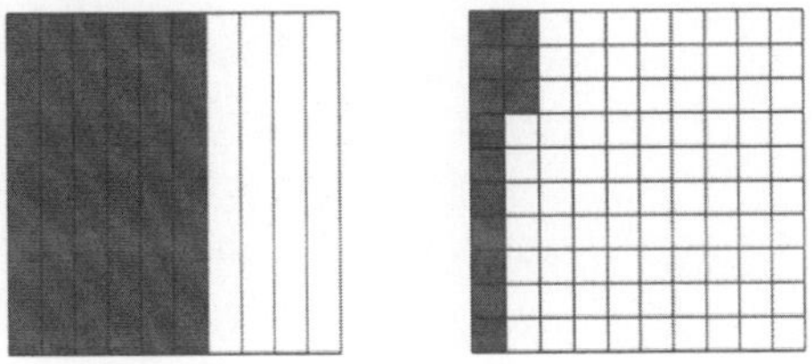

It is important to be aware of the **place value** when comparing decimal values. For example, consider the place value when comparing 0.3 and 0.03. Both values contain a 3, but one represents 3 tenths and the other represents 3 hundredths. Notice how $\frac{3}{10}$ covers more of the model than $\frac{3}{100}$.

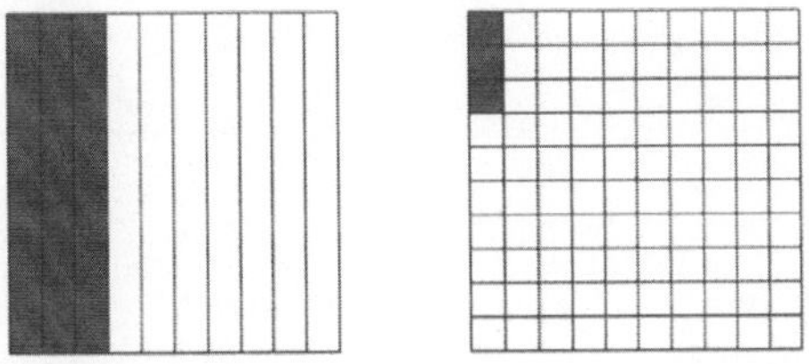

Relating Decimals to Fractions

Converting Decimals to Fractions

Decimals and fractions can be used to represent values less than one whole. Remember, one decimal place value to the right of the decimal point represents tenths, and two decimal places to the right of the decimal point represents hundredths. For example, 0.4 represents 4 tenths, or as a fraction $\frac{4}{10}$. The number 0.04 represents 4 hundredths, or as a fraction $\frac{4}{100}$.

When a decimal extends to the tenths place, the fraction has a denominator of 10.

$$0.1 = \frac{1}{10}$$

$$0.2 = \frac{2}{10}$$

$$0.3 = \frac{3}{10}$$

$$0.4 = \frac{4}{10}$$

When a decimal extends to the hundredths place, the fraction has a denominator of 100.

$$0.45 = \frac{45}{100}$$

$$0.35 = \frac{35}{100}$$

$$0.25 = \frac{25}{100}$$

$$0.15 = \frac{15}{100}$$

Equivalent Decimals and Fractions

Notice how $\frac{40}{100}$ and $\frac{4}{10}$ cover the **same amount** of the model. This means that $\frac{40}{100}$ and $\frac{4}{10}$ are **equivalent** fractions. Since $\frac{40}{100}$ and $\frac{4}{10}$ are equivalent fractions, 0.40 and 0.4 are equivalent decimals.

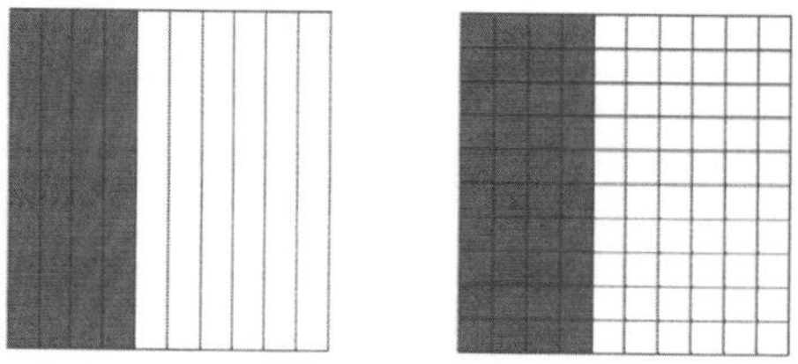

Here are some other examples of equivalent fractions and decimals:

$$\frac{1}{10} = 0.1 = 0.10 = \frac{10}{100}$$

$$\frac{2}{10} = 0.2 = 0.20 = \frac{20}{100}$$

$$\frac{3}{10} = 0.3 = 0.30 = \frac{30}{100}$$

Example

Express "45 hundredths" as a decimal and a fraction in simplest form.

45 hundredths represents 45 out of 100, which as a fraction is $\frac{45}{100}$. This fraction can be simplified. 45 and 100 have a factor in common. Divide both the numerator and denominator by the common factor of 5. $\frac{45}{100}$ becomes $\frac{9}{20}$.

$\frac{45}{100}$ can be expressed as a decimal. $\frac{45}{100}$ can be thought of as 4 tenths plus 5 hundredths. $\frac{4}{10}$ and $\frac{5}{100}$ is expressed as 0.45 in decimal form: $\frac{45}{100} = 0.45$.

45 hundredths as a decimal and a fraction: 0.45 and $\frac{9}{20}$.

EXAMPLE

Draw lines to connect the fraction and decimal values that are equivalent.

0.7	$\frac{6}{100}$
$\frac{2}{100}$	0.8
0.06	0.99
$\frac{99}{100}$	$\frac{7}{10}$
$\frac{4}{5}$	0.02

0.7 represents 7 tenths. As a fraction 0.7 is $\frac{7}{10}$.

$\frac{2}{100}$ represents 2 hundredths. As a decimal $\frac{2}{100}$ is 0.02.

0.06 represents 6 hundredths. As a fraction 0.06 is $\frac{6}{100}$.

$\frac{99}{100}$ represents 99 hundredths. As a decimal $\frac{99}{100}$ is 0.99.

$\frac{4}{5}$ represents 4 fifths, or 8 tenths. As a decimal $\frac{4}{5}$ is 0.8.

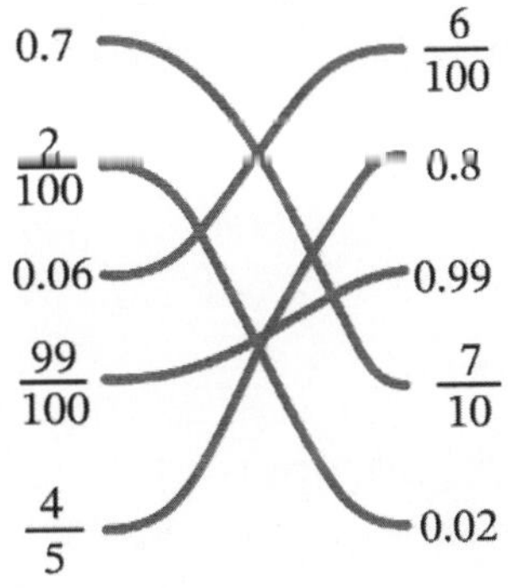

DECIMALS ON A NUMBER LINE

A number line is a great way to visualize decimals to the tenths or the hundredths places. On a number line, tenths show 10 equal segments from 0 to 1. Notice how the hash marks increase by 0.1 from left to right. The left dot is on the third hash mark, so it represents 0.3 or $\frac{3}{10}$. The right dot is on the ninth hash mark, so it represents 0.9 or $\frac{9}{10}$.

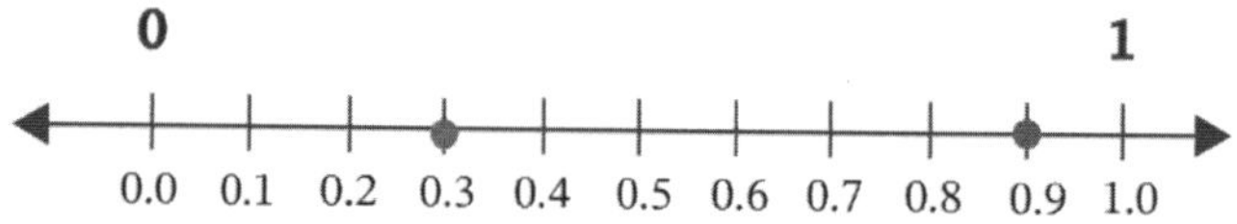

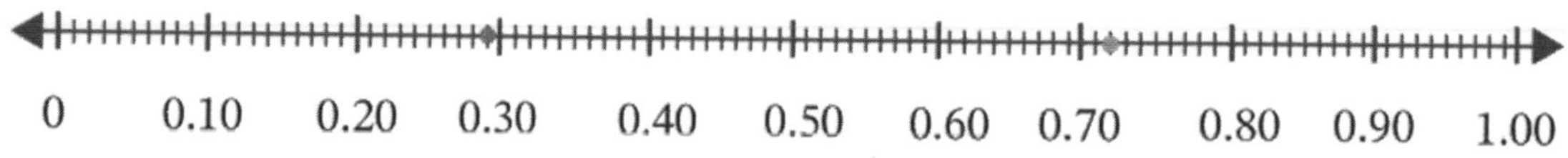

Hundredths show 100 equal segments from 0 to 100.

The left dot is on the 29th hash mark, so it represents $\frac{29}{100}$. The fraction $\frac{29}{100}$ as a decimal is 0.29. The orange dot is on the 72nd hash mark, so it represents $\frac{72}{100}$. The fraction $\frac{72}{100}$ as a decimal is 0.72.

Fractions

Unit Fractions

A **unit fraction** is any fraction with a numerator of 1. For example, $\frac{1}{2}, \frac{1}{3}, \frac{1}{4}$, and $\frac{1}{5}$ are considered unit fractions. When a unit fraction is added to itself multiple times, the result is a larger fraction. For example, $\frac{1}{8}+\frac{1}{8}+\frac{1}{8}=\frac{3}{8}$.

The opposite of this is **decomposing** a fraction into the sum of its unit fractions.

$\frac{5}{6}$ is the result of combining $\frac{1}{6}$ five times.

$$\frac{5}{6}=\frac{1}{6}+\frac{1}{6}+\frac{1}{6}+\frac{1}{6}+\frac{1}{6}$$

This is true for **mixed numbers** and **improper** fractions as well. Mixed numbers are values that are written using a whole number and a fraction. For example, $2\frac{1}{3}$ is a mixed number that consists of 7 groups of $\frac{1}{3}$.

$$2\frac{1}{3}=\frac{1}{3}+\frac{1}{3}+\frac{1}{3}+\frac{1}{3}+\frac{1}{3}+\frac{1}{3}+\frac{1}{3}$$

Improper fractions are fractions that have a numerator that is greater than the denominator. $\frac{4}{3}$ is an improper fraction that consists of 4 groups of $\frac{1}{3}$.

$$\frac{4}{3}=\frac{1}{3}+\frac{1}{3}+\frac{1}{3}+\frac{1}{3}$$

Decomposing Fractions

When a fraction is decomposed, it is **split up** into **smaller** fractions. The sum of these smaller fractions is the original fraction. For example, $\frac{7}{8}$ can be split up into the sum of $\frac{1}{8} + \frac{1}{8} + \frac{1}{8} + \frac{1}{8} + \frac{1}{8} + \frac{1}{8} + \frac{1}{8}$. However, this is not the only way to decompose $\frac{7}{8}$.

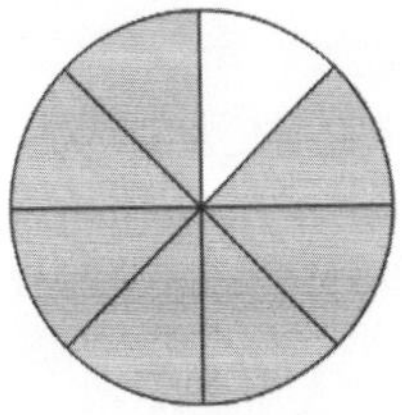

For example, the model below shows 7 shaded shares out of 8, or the fraction $\frac{7}{8}$. The fraction $\frac{7}{8}$ can be created in many ways. For example, $\frac{2}{8} + \frac{4}{8} + \frac{1}{8}$ has a sum of $\frac{7}{8}$.

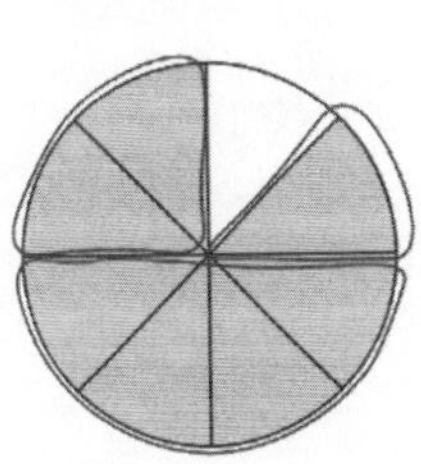

Equivalent Fractions

Fractions are considered **equivalent** if they represent the same amount. There are a few ways to determine if fractions are equivalent.

Models

Fractions can be compared by drawing a quick sketch. For example, consider the fractions $\frac{6}{8}$ and $\frac{3}{4}$. Create two circles that are the same size. Divide one circle into 8 equal shares, and the other circle into 4 equal shares. Notice how 6 out of 8 is the same size as 3 out of 4. Since $\frac{6}{8}$ and $\frac{3}{4}$ cover the same amount of each circle, they are considered equivalent. Creating a sketch or a model is a great way to compare fractions with denominators that are small. However, when denominators are larger, like $\frac{1}{40}$ or $\frac{39}{100}$, a sketch is unreasonable.

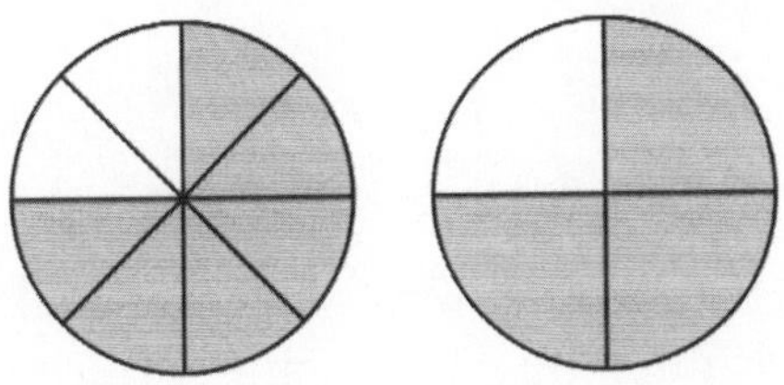

Common Denominators

For larger denominators, consider using a common denominator to determine if fractions are equivalent. For example, consider the fractions $\frac{46}{100}$ and $\frac{70}{150}$. The fractions cannot be compared until they have the same denominator. The lowest common multiple of 100 and 150 is 300. Set up each fraction with 300 as the denominator.

$\frac{46}{100}$ becomes $\frac{x}{300}$.

$\frac{70}{150}$ becomes $\frac{y}{300}$.

Now adjust the numerators.

$\frac{46}{100}$: The denominator is multiplied by 3 to get 300, so multiply the numerator by 3 as well: $\frac{46\times3}{100\times3} = \frac{138}{300}$.

$\frac{70}{150}$: The denominator is multiplied by 2 to get 300, so multiply the numerator by 2 as well: $\frac{70\times2}{150\times2} = \frac{140}{300}$.

Now that the two fractions have the same denominator, they can be compared. $\frac{138}{300}$ is not equivalent to $\frac{140}{300}$ because the numerators are different while the denominators are the same.

Comparing Fractions

It can be difficult to compare fractions when the numerators and denominators are different. For example, consider the fractions $\frac{7}{9}$ and $\frac{8}{11}$. It is difficult to know which fraction is larger because one fraction is out of 9, and one fraction is out of 11. To compare these fractions, create a common denominator.

One denominator is 9, and the other is 11. A common denominator can be calculated by determining the least common multiple (LCM). The LCM of 9 and 11 is 99. Set up each fraction with 99 as the new denominator.

$\frac{7}{9}$ becomes $\frac{x}{99}$.

$\frac{8}{11}$ becomes $\frac{x}{99}$.

Now adjust the numerators.

The denominator in $\frac{7}{9}$ was multiplied by 11 to reach $\frac{x}{99}$. Multiply the numerator by 11 as well: $\frac{7\times11}{9\times11} = \frac{77}{99}$.

The denominator in $\frac{8}{11}$ was multiplied by 9 to reach $\frac{x}{99}$. Multiply the numerator by 9 as well: $\frac{8\times9}{11\times9} = \frac{72}{99}$.

Now the two new fractions can be compared. $\frac{77}{99}$ is greater than $\frac{72}{99}$, or $\frac{77}{99} > \frac{72}{99}$.

EXAMPLE

Fill in the blank to make the statement true. $\frac{3}{5}$ __ $\frac{2}{7}$

Use one of the following symbols: >, <, or =.

$\frac{3}{5}$ and $\frac{2}{7}$ have different denominators. To compare the fractions, rewrite each fraction with a common denominator. The lowest multiple that both 5 and 7 have in common is 35. Rewrite the fractions with 35 as the denominator.

$\frac{3}{5}$ becomes $\frac{?}{35}$

$\frac{2}{7}$ becomes $\frac{?}{35}$

Now adjust the numerators.

$\frac{3}{5}$: The denominator was 5 and now it is 35. 5 was multiplied by 7, so multiply the numerator by 7 as well. $\frac{3}{5}$ becomes $\frac{21}{35}$.

$\frac{2}{7}$: The denominator was 7 and now it is 35. 7 was multiplied by 5, so multiply the numerator by 5 as well. $\frac{2}{7}$ becomes $\frac{10}{35}$.

$\frac{21}{35} > \frac{10}{35}$, therefore $\frac{3}{5} > \frac{2}{7}$.

EXAMPLE

Compare the two fractions using the symbol >,<, or =: $\frac{5}{6}$ __ $\frac{7}{8}$.

The fractions $\frac{5}{6}$ and $\frac{7}{8}$ can be compared once they have a common denominator. Look at the denominators: 6 and 8. The lowest common multiple of 6 and 8 is 24. Make 24 the new denominator for both fractions.

$\frac{5}{6}$ becomes $\frac{?}{24}$

$\frac{7}{8}$ becomes $\frac{?}{24}$

Now adjust the numerators. What was the original denominator multiplied by? Multiply the numerator by this same amount.

$\frac{5}{6}$: The denominator was multiplied by 4 to create $\frac{?}{24}$. Multiply the numerator by 4. $\frac{5}{6}$ becomes $\frac{20}{24}$.

$\frac{7}{8}$: The denominator was multiplied by 3 to create $\frac{?}{24}$. Multiply the numerator by 3. $\frac{7}{8}$ becomes $\frac{21}{24}$.

$\frac{20}{24} < \frac{21}{24}$, therefore $\frac{5}{6} < \frac{7}{8}$.

Adding and Subtracting Fractions

Fractions represent part of a whole. Fractions with the same denominator can be combined by adding the parts (the numerators, or top numbers). This can be represented using a model. For example, the model below shows 3 parts out of 6, and 1 part out of 6. In other words, the whole model shows $\frac{3}{6} + \frac{1}{6}$.

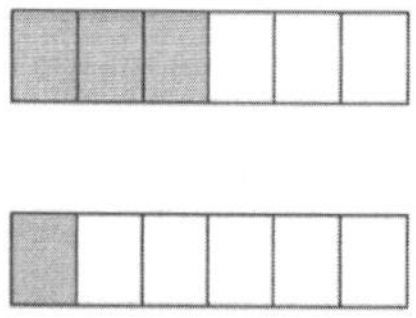

Both fractions consist of sixths, so the parts can be combined. 3 parts combined with 1 part equals 4 parts. 4 parts out of 6 parts represents the fraction $\frac{4}{6}$.

Try another example. Consider the diagram below. Each whole is divided into 8 equal shares. The circle on the left shows 2 out of 8, or $\frac{2}{8}$. The circle on the right shows 6 out of 8, or $\frac{6}{8}$.

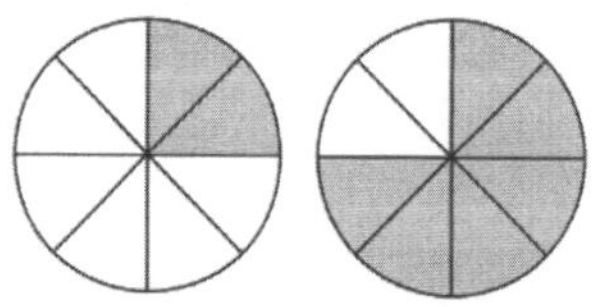

Both fractions have the same denominators so their numerators can be combined. $\frac{2}{8} + \frac{6}{8}$ combines to $\frac{8}{8}$. Another way to express $\frac{8}{8}$ is 1 whole.

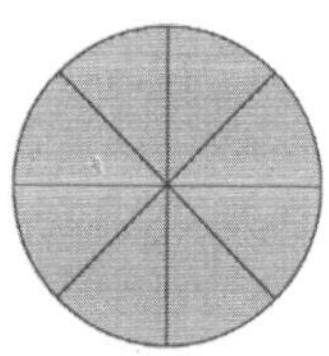

A picture or model is a great way to represent addition and subtraction of fractions. However, there is a shortcut! When denominators are the same, simply add or subtract the numerators.

$$\frac{2}{7} + \frac{4}{7} = \frac{6}{7}$$

Notice how the denominator, 7, stays the same and the numerators are added.

$$\frac{8}{9}-\frac{3}{9}=\frac{5}{9}$$

Notice how the denominator, 9, stays the same and the numerators are subtracted.

EXAMPLE

Write and solve an addition equation that represents adding the top fraction to the bottom fraction illustrated below.

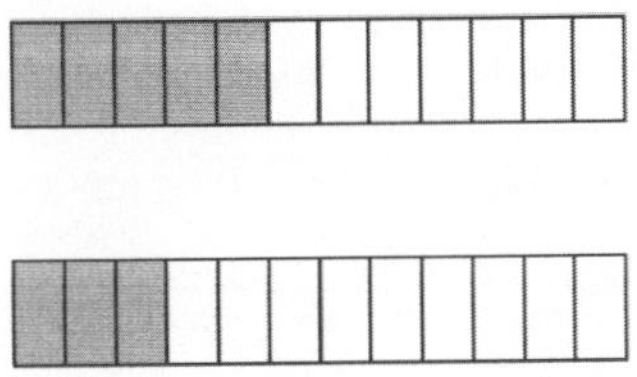

Top fraction: $\frac{5}{12}$

Bottom fraction: $\frac{3}{12}$

Both fractions have the same denominator, so they can be combined.

$$\frac{5}{12}+\frac{3}{12}=\frac{8}{12}$$

$\frac{8}{12}$ can be simplified by dividing the numerator and denominator by 4. $\frac{8}{12}$ becomes $\frac{2}{3}$.

$$\frac{5}{12}+\frac{3}{12}=\frac{8}{12}=\frac{2}{3}$$

EXAMPLE

Model the subtraction equation on the number line, then solve: $\frac{6}{10}-\frac{2}{10}=?$

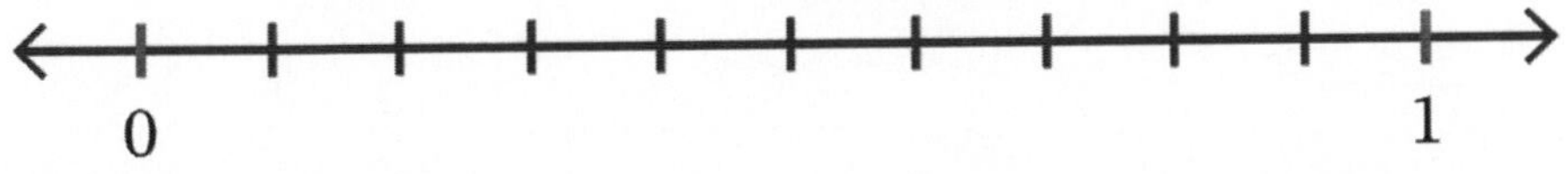

The number line is divided into 10 equal shares. Each hash mark represents $\frac{1}{10}$.

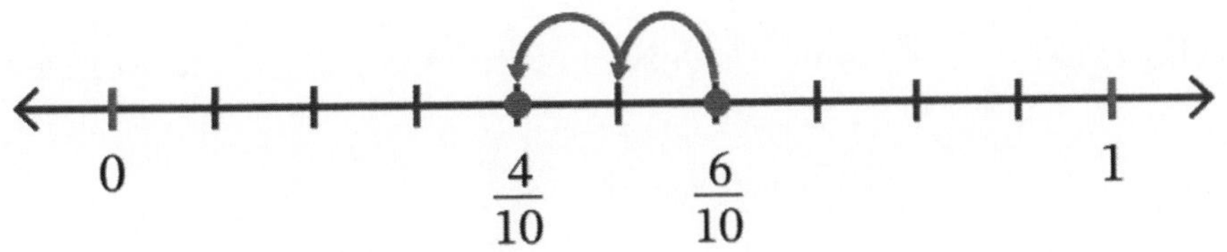

The red dot starts at $\frac{6}{10}$. The arrows show 2 jumps back, which represents subtraction of $\frac{2}{10}$: $\frac{6}{10}-\frac{2}{10}=\frac{4}{10}$.

Reasonable Sums and Differences of Fractions

One way to check whether or not the sums and differences of fractions are reasonable is to use benchmark fractions. **Benchmarks fractions** are common, easy to visualize fractions such as 0, $\frac{1}{4}$, $\frac{1}{2}$, $\frac{3}{4}$, and 1.

For example, consider the following addition equation:

$$\frac{1}{12}+\frac{7}{12}=\frac{8}{12}$$

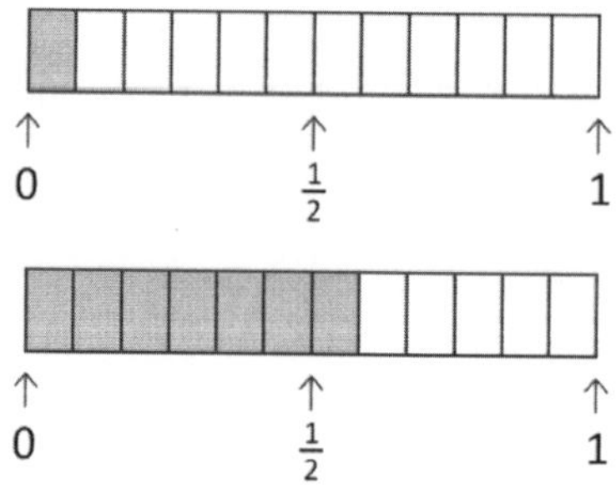

Notice how $\frac{1}{12}$ is close to the benchmark fraction 0, and $\frac{7}{12}$ is close to the benchmark fraction $\frac{1}{2}$. Since $0+\frac{1}{2}=\frac{1}{2}$, the sum of $\frac{1}{12}$ and $\frac{7}{12}$ should be close to $\frac{1}{2}$.

$\frac{1}{12}+\frac{7}{12}=\frac{8}{12}$, and $\frac{8}{12}$ is close to $\frac{1}{2}$ since it's only one more shaded square from our picture earlier, so the sum is reasonable.

The same concept works for fractions with unequal denominators. For example, $\frac{7}{10}-\frac{2}{8}=\frac{9}{20}$. The reasonableness of the answer can be determined without solving the problem. From our picture, we can see that $\frac{7}{10}$ is close to $\frac{3}{4}$, and $\frac{2}{8}$ is the same as $\frac{1}{4}$. Therefore, the difference should be close to $\frac{3}{4}-\frac{1}{4}$ which is $\frac{2}{4}$, or $\frac{1}{2}$.

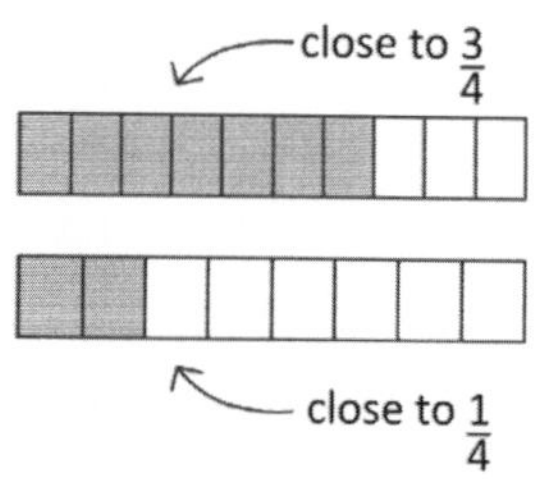

The equation shows $\frac{7}{10}-\frac{2}{8}=\frac{9}{20}$, and $\frac{9}{20}$ is very close to $\frac{2}{4}$ or $\frac{1}{2}$, so the answer seems to be reasonable.

Multiplying Fractions and Whole Numbers

Modeling strategies can be helpful when multiplying a whole number by a fraction. For example, $4 \times \frac{2}{3}$ can be thought of as 4 groups of $\frac{2}{3}$. There are 8 thirds altogether, so $4 \times \frac{2}{3} = \frac{8}{3}$, or as a mixed number, $2\frac{2}{3}$.

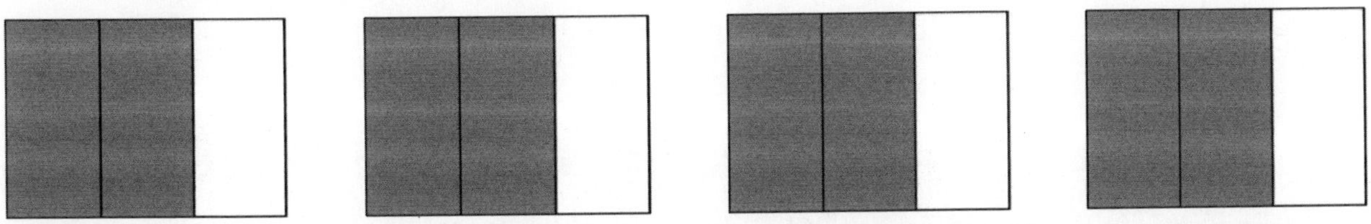

Multiplication is commutative, meaning the order does not matter. This same modeling strategy applies in situations where the fraction is listed first and the whole number is listed second.

Decimals and Fractions on a Number Line

Fractions with a denominator of 10 can be represented as a decimal value to the tenths place. For example, $\frac{9}{10}$ written as a decimal is 0.9.

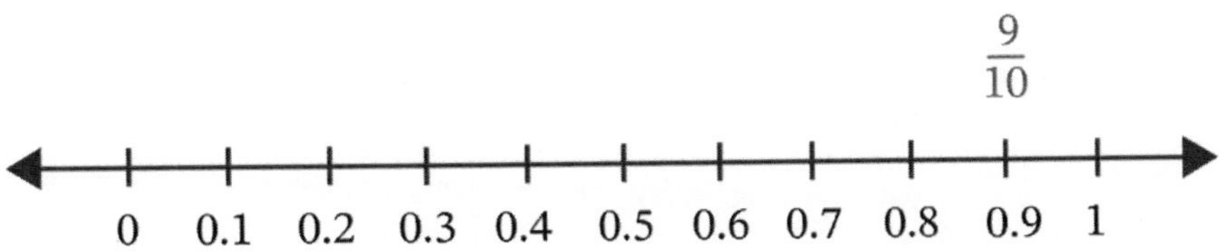

Similarly, fractions with a denominator of 100 can be represented as a decimal value to the hundredth place. For example, $\frac{9}{100}$ is 0.09 as a decimal.

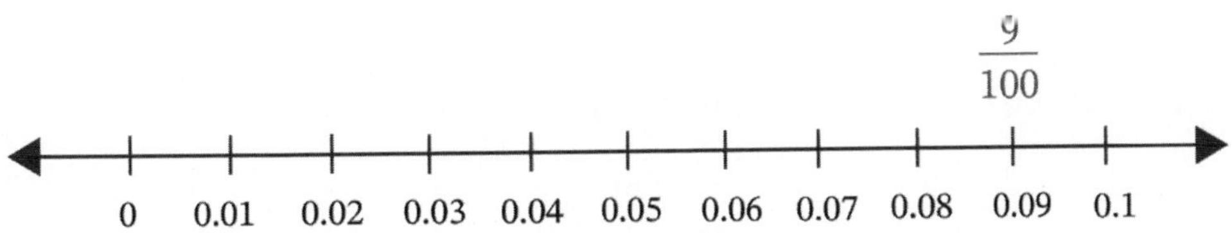

Decimals and fractions can be thought of as distances from zero on a number line. In general, the number line will extend from 0 to 1, where 1 represents 1 whole. Decimal and fraction values often represent values that are greater than 0 but less than 1 whole.

When a number line is not labeled, look for the number of equal segments. The number line below has 10 equal segments, which means each hash mark represents $\frac{1}{10}$. The dot is located on the eighth hash mark, so it represents $\frac{8}{10}$. The fraction $\frac{8}{10}$ represents the decimal 0.8 or 0.80. These values, $\frac{8}{10}$, 0.8, and 0.80, all represent the distance from zero.

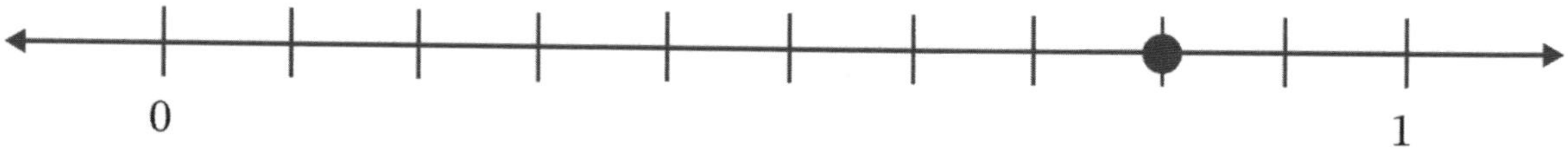

Adding and Subtracting Decimals and Whole Numbers

The important thing to remember when adding and subtracting decimal numbers is to **line up** the **decimal points**. Lining up the decimal points ensures that similar place values are being combined. For example, ones combine with ones, tens combine with tens.

Consider the following: A pizza costs \$27.50 and a drink costs \$4.65. The total cost of the meal can be calculated by finding the sum. Stack the numbers vertically and line up the decimal points. With addition, it does not matter which number is on top or bottom. Regroup if necessary and bring the decimal straight down into the answer line. This method is known as the **standard algorithm**.

$$\begin{array}{r} {\scriptstyle 11} \\ 27.50 \\ +\ 4.65 \\ \hline \$32.15 \end{array}$$

The standard algorithm is also useful for subtraction scenarios. For example, if a piece of ribbon measures 132.1 centimeters, and 27.76 centimeters are cut off and removed, how many centimeters of ribbon are left?

Stack the values vertically and line up the decimals. Make sure the larger number, 132.1, is on the top. Sometimes it is helpful to fill in any empty spaces with a zero. Regroup if necessary, and again bring the decimal straight down into the answer line.

$$\begin{array}{r} 1\ \ \ 1\ \\ 1\ \ \ 0\ \\ \ \ \ 1 \\ 2\ \not{1}\ \ \not{0}\ 0 \\ 1\ \not{3}\ \not{2}\ .\ \not{1}\ \not{0} \\ -\ \ \ 2\ 7\ .\ 7\ 6 \\ \hline 1\ 0\ 4\ .\ 3\ 4 \end{array}$$

There are 104.34 centimeters of ribbon left.

Review Video: Adding and Subtracting Decimals
Visit mometrix.com/academy and enter code: 381101

EXAMPLE

Solve using the standard algorithm: 40.03 − 26.12 = ____

Line up the decimals when adding and subtracting decimals. Regrouping is required for this problem.

$$\begin{array}{r} \overset{3}{\cancel{4}}\overset{\overset{9}{\cancel{10}}}{\cancel{0}}.\overset{10}{\cancel{0}}3 \\ -26.12 \\ \hline 13.91 \end{array}$$

40.03 − 26.12 = 13.91

Check for accuracy using addition: 13.91 + 26.12 = 40.03.

EXAMPLE

Solve using the standard algorithm: 63.04 + 99.09 = ____.

$$\begin{array}{r} \overset{1}{6}3.\overset{1}{0}4 \\ +99.09 \\ \hline 162.13 \end{array}$$

Line up the decimals when adding and subtracting decimals: 63.04 + 99.09 = 162.13.

Measurement and Data

Measuring Angles

A **protractor** is a tool that is used to measure the **exact degree measure** of any angle. A protractor has two rows of degree measures, an inside row and an outside row. It is important to remember to use the row that starts at 0° when measuring angles. The row that is selected depends on the direction the angle opens. For example, notice how the protractor on the left shows an angle that opens to the right. The baseline on the right starts at 0° using the inside row of numbers. In contrast, the protractor on the right shows an angle that opens to the left. The baseline on the left starts at 0° using the outside row of numbers.

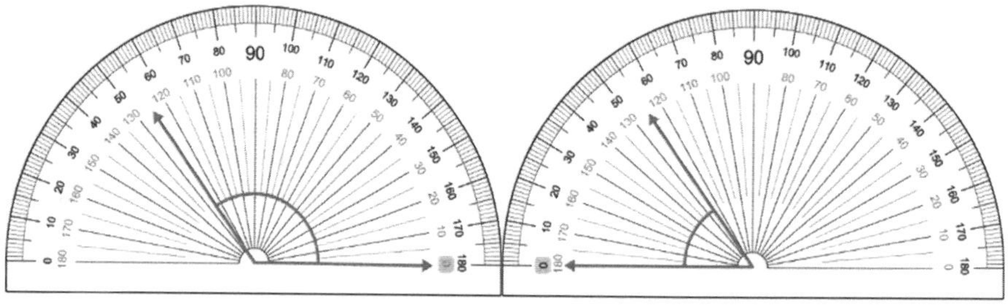

When using a protractor to measure an angle, identify the row of degree measures that start at 0°, and build the angle from there. For example, the angle below is built from two rays. The mouth of the angle opens to the right, so the inside row of numbers will be used. Starting at 0°, the angle extends all the way to 65°.

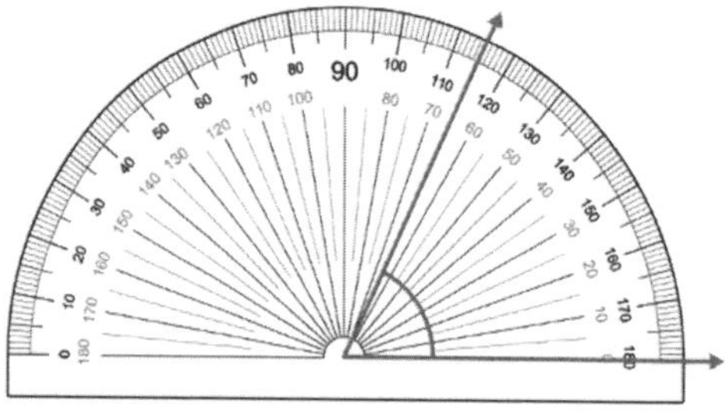

Example

Use a protractor to determine the angle measure below.

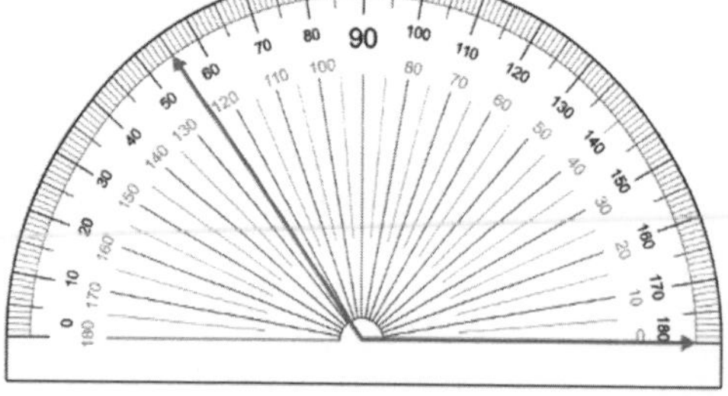

A protractor can be used to measure the obtuse angle. The angle is 125°.

EXAMPLE

Is the following angle greater or less than 85°?

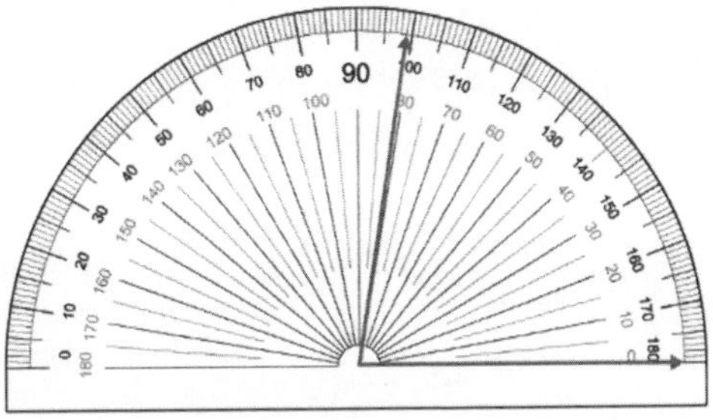

Less than. The angle above is an 81° angle.

Drawing Angles

Before drawing an angle with a given measure, consider visualizing the angle using **benchmark angles**, which are angles that are commonly known. Will the angle be close to 90°? Will the angle be close to 0° or 180°? This can be a helpful way to check the accuracy of the angle that is drawn.

For example, to draw a 55° angle, start by using a straightedge to draw the baseline of the angle. A 55° angle will be somewhere between the benchmark of 45° and 90°. Line up the baseline of the protractor with the line that is drawn. Follow the degree measures from 0° to 55° and make a small mark or dot at 55°. Now connect the baseline to the new dot/mark at 55°. The result is an angle that is 55°.

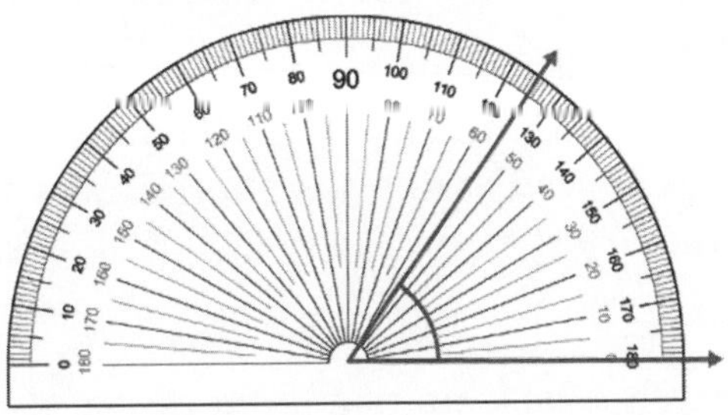

Solving for Unknown Angle Measurements

When an unknown angle is formed from a **benchmark angle**, such as 180° or 90°, **subtraction** can be used to determine the missing angle. For example, the angle below shows a 90° angle formed by two adjacent angles. The sum of the 40° angle and the unknown angle need to combine to form a 90° angle.

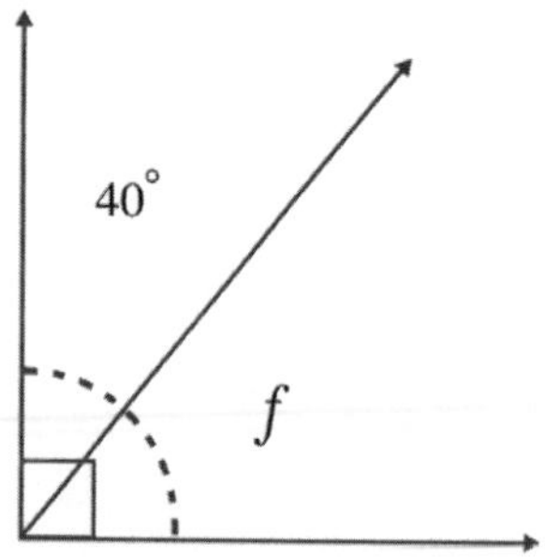

$$f = 90° - 40° = 50°$$

Adjacent angles won't always combine to form benchmark angles. For example, the adjacent angles below don't combine to form a benchmark angle. However, both angles combine to 120°. This means that angle $\angle a + \angle b = 120°$. $\angle a$ is 62°, so an addition equation can be set up.

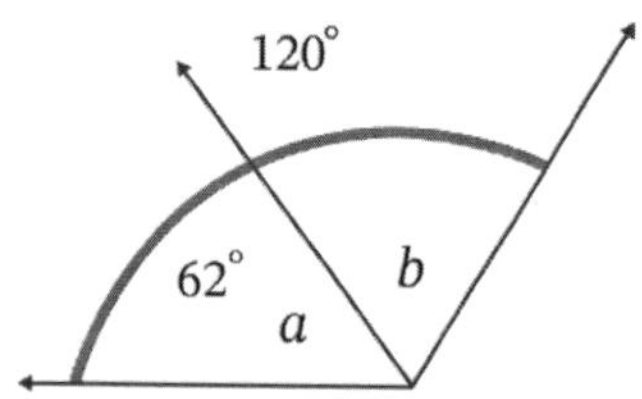

$$b = 120° - 62°$$
$$b = 58°$$

Relative Sizes of Measurements

The **metric system** is a system of measurement used for identifying mass, volume, and length. Most countries in the world use the metric system when making calculations in math and science. However, the United States has another measurement system called the **customary system**. The customary system also measures mass, volume, and length, but it uses different units.

For example, the metric system has base units of meters, liters, and grams. Meters measure length, liters measure volume, and grams measure mass. The metric system is convenient in math and science because it follows the base-ten number system. This means that quick calculations and conversions can be done simply by multiplying or dividing by a power of ten. For example, 10 millimeters is equivalent to 1 centimeter.

The customary system has much more than three units. For example, when measuring volume, options include ounces, cups, pints, quarts, and gallons. Converting between units is more challenging because each unit has a different conversion factor. For example, there are 4 quarts in a gallon, but 16 ounces in a pint. Distance is measured in inches, feet, yards, and miles. Mass is similar to weight, and is measured in ounces, pounds, and tons. It is important to become familiar with units in the metric and customary systems.

Customary Units

- **1 ounce**: about the weight of a candy bar
- **1 pound**: about the weight of a football
- **1 ton**: about the weight of a car

- **1 inch**: about the width of a quarter
- **1 foot**: about the height of a 2 liter soda bottle (12 inches)
- **1 yard**: about the width of a door (3 feet)
- **1 mile**: about 4 laps on an outdoor running track

- **1 ounce**: the amount of liquid in two tablespoons
- **1 cup**: the amount of liquid in a coffee cup (8 ounces)
- **1 pint**: the amount of liquid in a small water bottle (16 ounces)
- **1 quart**: the amount of liquid in a jug of juice (2 pints)
- **1 gallon**: the amount of liquid in a large container of milk

Metric Units

- **Meter:** about the width of a door frame
- **Liter:** about the volume of a large water bottle
- **Gram:** about the mass of a paperclip

Converting Between Units

Metric System

When converting units within the metric system, simply multiply or divide by a factor of 10. Notice the base unit is bolded (1 meter, 1 gram and 1 liter).

Length	Weight	Volume
1 km = 1,000 m	1 kg = 1,000 g	1 kL = 1,000 L
1 m = 0.001 km	1 g = 0.001 kg	1 L = 0.001 kL
1 m = 100 cm	**1 g** = 100 cg	**1 L** = 100 cL
1 cm = 0.01 m	1 cg = 0.01 g	1 cL = 0.01 L
1 m = 1,000 mm	1 g = 1,000 mg	1 L = 1,000 mL
1 mm = 0.001 m	1 mg = 0.001 g	1 mL = 0.001 L

For example, 2.56 meters is equivalent to 256 centimeters because meters are 100 times larger than centimeters. 3,366 millimeters is equivalent to 3.366 meters because millimeters are 1,000 times smaller than meters. Conversions in the metric system are quick because all it requires is knowing where to move the decimal point. Remember, each decimal movement to the right represents multiplication by 10. Each decimal movement to the left represents division by 10.

Review Video: Metric System Conversion
Visit mometrix.com/academy and enter code: 163709

Customary System

Converting within the customary system is more complicated. For this reason, the metric system is generally the system used in math and science. Notice how there is not really any pattern to follow when converting from one unit to the next. For example, there are 5,280 feet in a mile, but there are 12 inches in a foot.

Length	Weight	Volume
12 in = 1 ft	16 oz = 1 lb	128 fl. oz = 1 gal
3 ft = 1yd	2,000 lb = 1 ton	2 pt = 1 qt
5,280 ft = 1 mi		8 pt = 1 gal
1,760 yd = 1 mi		4 qt = 1 gal

Solving Problems Involving Measurements

When solving problems involving units for mass, length, or volume, first identify whether the units are metric or customary. Once this has been determined, think about how much you will need to multiply or divide by to make the **conversion**. For example, consider the following scenario.

James is pouring 4 gallons of juice into pints. How many pints can James pour if he pours out all the juice?

Ask yourself, "are these customary or metric units?" These are customary units.

Now, consider how many pints are in 4 gallons. There are 4 quarts in a gallon, so there are 16 quarts total.

There are 8 pints in a quart, so there are 16×8 total pints.

$$16 \times 8 = 128$$

James can pour 128 pints of juice.

Example

A baseball game started at 7:10. The game ended at 9:15. How long did the game last?

Count up by hours and then count up by minutes. 7:10 to 8:10 is one hour. 8:10 to 9:10 is one hour. 9:10 to 9:15 is 5 minutes. Altogether, this is 2 hours and 5 minutes.

Example

A tablet weighs 265 grams. Does a stack of 8 of these tablets have a mass that is more or less than 1 kilogram? (1 kg = 1,000 g)

Each tablet has a mass of 265 grams, so 8 tablets have a mass of $8 \times 265\text{ g} = 2{,}120\text{ kg}$. The mass of 8 tablets is 2,120 grams. 1 kilogram consists of 1,000 grams. $2{,}120 > 1{,}000$, so the tablets have a mass greater than 1 kilogram.

Solving Using the Area and Perimeter of Rectangles

The **area** of a rectangle is calculated by multiplying the **length** and the **width**. For example, the rectangle below has a length of 8 yards and a width of 3 yards. So, the area of the rectangle is $8 \times 3 = 24$ square yards.

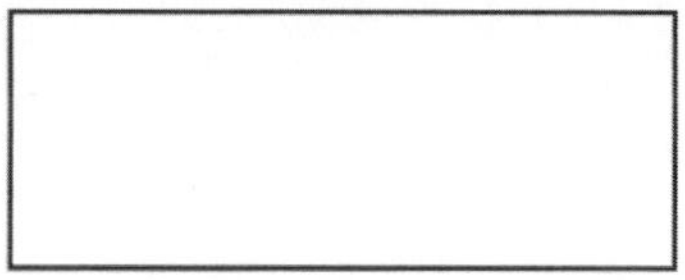

The **perimeter** of a rectangle is calculated by adding all four **side lengths**.

$$\text{Perimeter} = \text{length} + \text{length} + \text{width} + \text{width}$$

Another way to calculate perimeter: $P = 2l + 2w$.

A rectangle has 2 lengths and 2 widths, and the sum of these 4 sides is the perimeter. For example, the rectangle below has a length of 32 meters and a width of 20 meters.

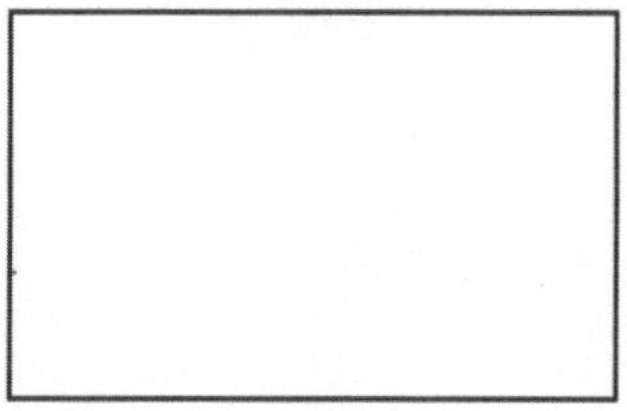

$$P = 32 + 32 + 20 + 20$$

$$P = (2 \times 32) + (2 \times 20)$$

Both equations simplify to 104, so the perimeter of the rectangle is 104 meters.

Variation in Rectangle Construction

A group of rectangles can have the same area but different perimeters. For example, consider a rectangle with an area of 20 square feet. How can this rectangle be built?

The rectangle may have a length of 1 foot and a width of 20 feet.

The rectangle may have a length of 2 feet and a width of 10 feet.

The rectangle may have a length of 4 feet and a width of 5 feet.

All three of these rectangles have an area of 20 square feet. However, each rectangle has a unique perimeter.

1 foot by 20 feet: Perimeter of 42 feet.

2 feet by 10 feet: Perimeter of 24 feet.

4 feet by 5 feet: Perimeter of 18 feet.

Now, consider a rectangle with a perimeter of 10 meters. There is more than one correct way to build this rectangle. For example, a 3-meter by 2-meter rectangle has a perimeter of 10 meters and an area of 6 square meters. However, a 4-meter by 1-meter rectangle also has a perimeter of 10 meters but it has an area of 4 square meters.

Review Video: Area and Perimeter of Rectangles and Squares
Visit mometrix.com/academy and enter code: 428109

EXAMPLE

A city planner is creating a model design for new green space. The model has an area of 96 square centimeters and a length of 12 centimeters. What is the width of the model?

The area of a rectangle is calculated by multiplying the length by the width: $A = l \times w$. In this scenario, the area and the length are provided. Substitute A and l into the formula.

$$A = l \times w$$

$$96 = 12 \times w$$

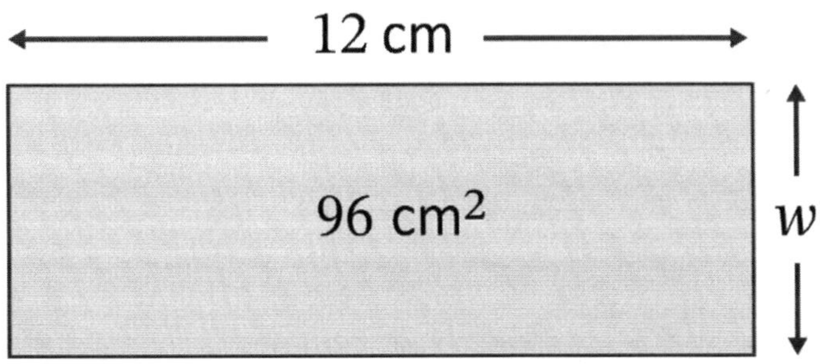

Divide 96 by 12 to find the width.

$$w = 96 \div 12 = 8$$

The width of the model is 8 centimeters.

EXAMPLE

Student A says there is only one way to draw a rectangle with a perimeter of 14 units. Student B says there is more than one way do draw a rectangle with a perimeter of 14 units. Which student is correct? Support your answer with a model.

Option 1: 2 by 5. This rectangle has an area of 10 square units and a perimeter of 14 units.

Option 2: 1 by 6. This rectangle has an area of 6 square units and a perimeter of 14 units.

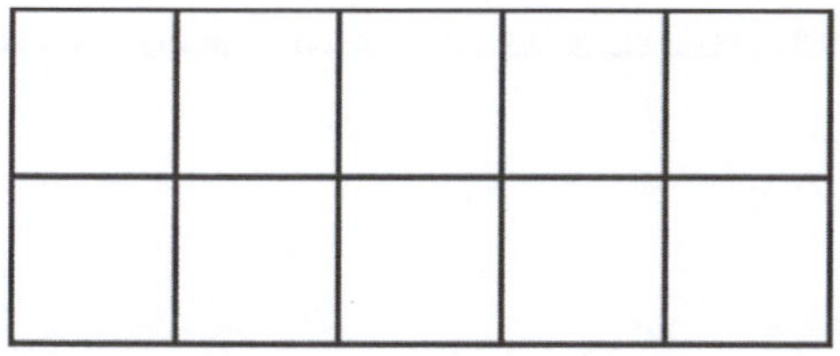

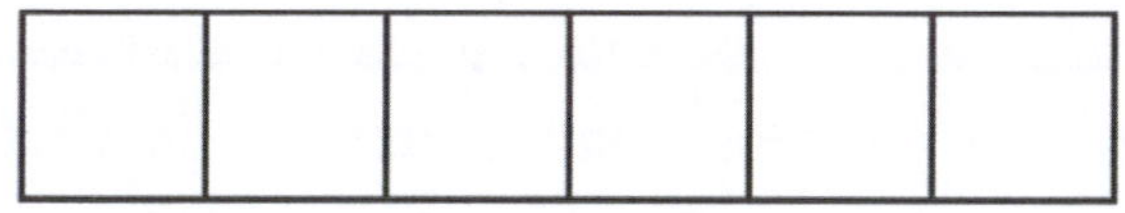

Student B is correct. There is more than one way to draw a rectangle with a perimeter of 14 units.

Dot Plot

A **dot plot** is a graph that uses dots above a number line to show the frequency of data. For example, the dot plot on the left shows how many books were read last summer by different students. The number of dots corresponds to the number of books each student read. 4 students read 0 books, 6 students read 1 book, and so on. The dot plot on the right shows the number of cups of different ingredients used in a pancake recipe. This dot plot shows that there is a total of $2\frac{5}{6}$ cups of ingredients needed for this recipe.

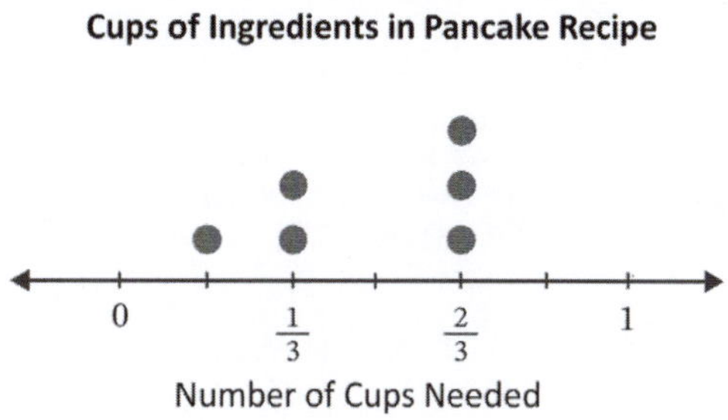

Example

A group of students have started a book club. The display below shows the progress each student has made reading the assigned book. Each X represents 1 student. How many students have read more than half of the book? How many students have read exactly half of the book so far?

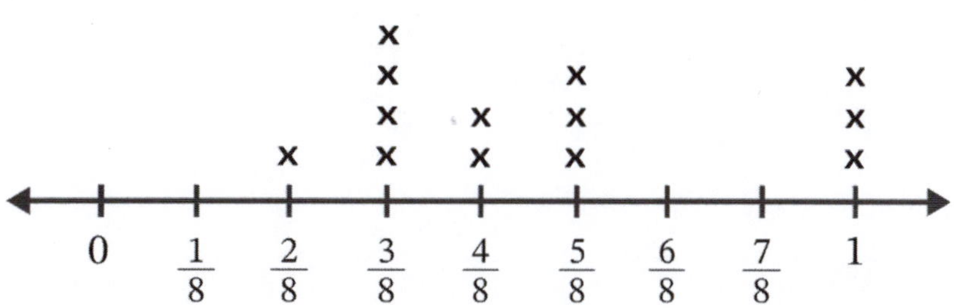

Each X represents 1 student. $\frac{4}{8}$ represents half of the book, and there are 2 Xs on $\frac{4}{8}$. This means 2 students have read exactly half of the book. There are 3 Xs on $\frac{5}{8}$ and 3 Xs on 1. This means that 6 students have read more than half of the book.

Geometry

Geometry Terms

Geometry, or the study of shapes, is filled with unique terminology and vocabulary. It is important to become familiar with this math vocabulary to be able to precisely classify and identify two- and three-dimensional shapes.

The most basic terms include points, lines, line segments, rays, angles, perpendicular lines, and parallel lines.

A **point** is an exact location with no size. This often appears as a dot, and is usually labeled with a letter, such as Point *A*.

Point *A*

A **line** is a straight path that extends in opposite directions. A line does not have a width, and it extends indefinitely in both directions. Lines are labeled with letters representing points on the line, such as $\overleftrightarrow{AB}$.

$\overleftrightarrow{AB}$

A **line segment** is a part of a line. A line segment has endpoints, beginning and ending at a point labeled with a letter, such as $\overline{AB}$.

AB

A **ray** is a part of a line that starts at an endpoint and then extends out indefinitely. Rays are labeled starting with a letter at the endpoint and ending with a letter representing another point on the ray, such as $\overrightarrow{AB}$.

$\overrightarrow{AB}$

An **angle** is formed when two straight lines or rays meet at a common endpoint. The two rays below form an angle.

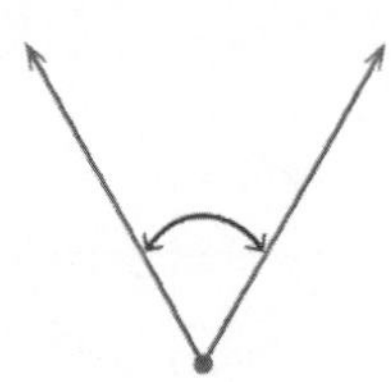

Parallel lines extend side-by-side and never intersect. To help visualize parallel lines, think of train tracks.

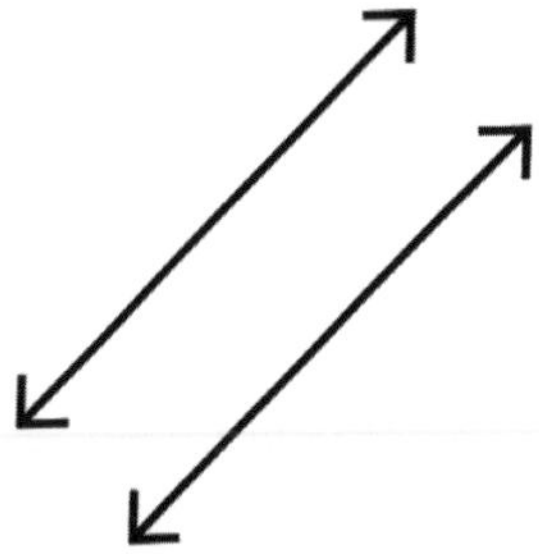

Perpendicular lines intersect to form a right angle. To help visualize perpendicular lines, think of a corner or a T-shape.

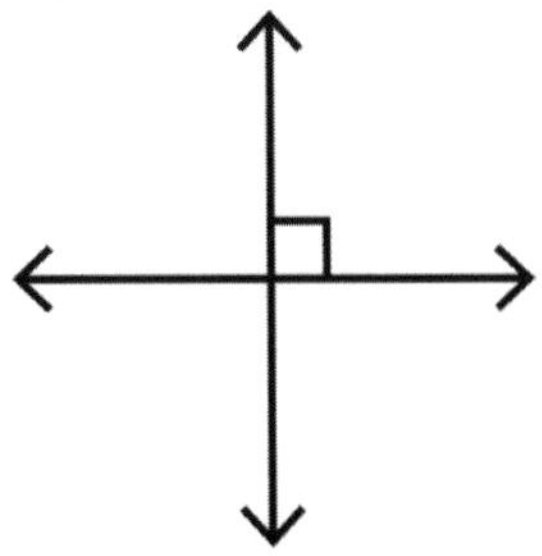

Review Video: Parallel and Perpendicular Lines
Visit mometrix.com/academy and enter code: 815923

Lines of Symmetry

A **line of symmetry** is a line that can be drawn through a two-dimensional shape so that each side of the line is a **reflection** of the other. If a mirror was placed on this line, the reflection would **exactly** match on both sides of the line. Some two-dimensional shapes one line of symmetry, some have more than one line of symmetry, and some shapes have no lines of symmetry.

For example, consider the two-dimensional shapes below.

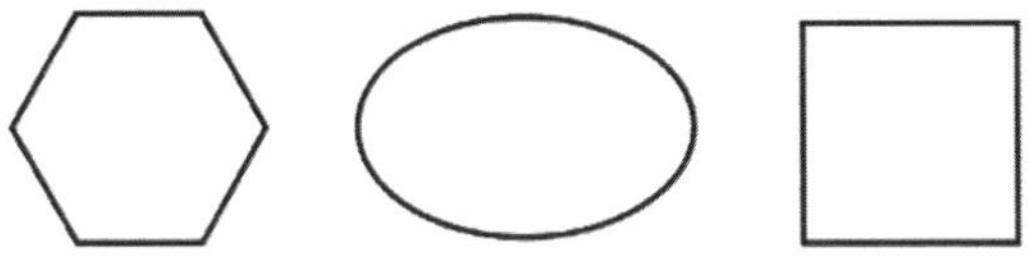

The hexagon will have 6 lines of symmetry, the oval will have 2 lines of symmetry, and the square will have 4 lines of symmetry.

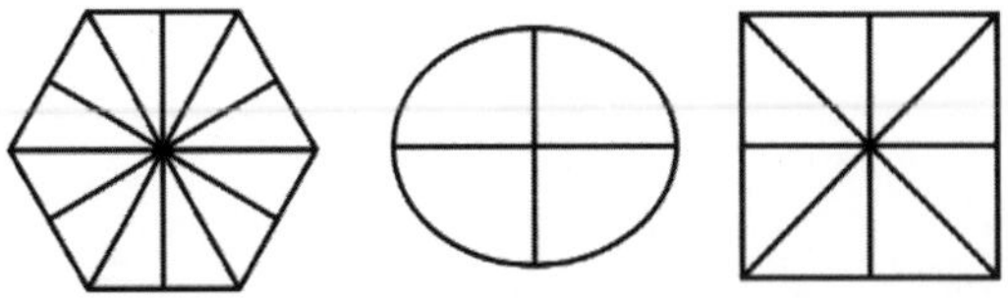

If each shape is folded on one of the lines, the resulting shape will line up in a way that has no overlaps.

Some two-dimensional shapes will not have a line of symmetry. For example, consider the parallelogram below.

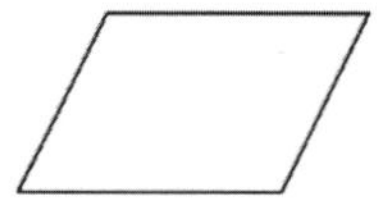

It may look like there is a way to fold this parallelogram without creating overhangs, but there is not. This indicates that there are no lines of symmetry.

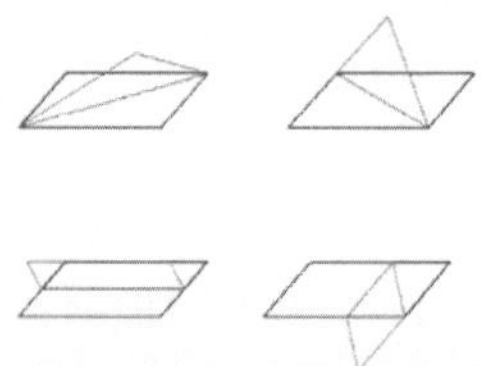

Review Video: Symmetry
Visit mometrix.com/academy and enter code: 528106

Right, Acute, and Obtuse Angles

A **right angle** consists of 90 degrees and forms a corner. Angles that are less than 90 degrees are considered **acute angles**. Angles that are wider than 90 degrees but less than 180 degrees are considered **obtuse angles**.

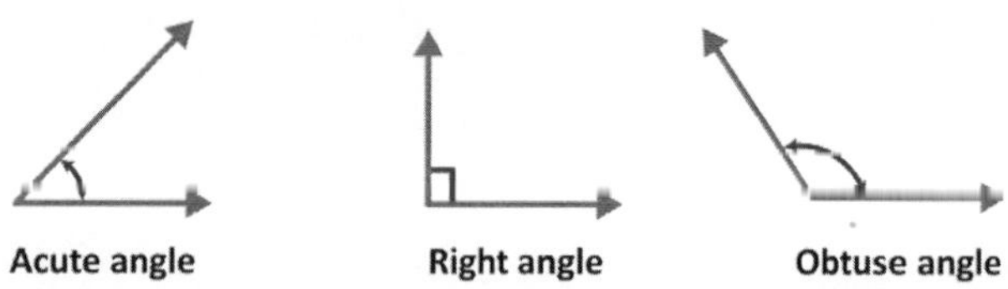

Triangles can be built from acute, obtuse, or right angles. For example, a triangle with only acute angles is referred to as an **acute triangle**. A triangle with an obtuse angle is called an **obtuse triangle**. A triangle containing a right angle is called a **right triangle**.

Triangle 1 contains a 90-degree angle, so it is classified as a right triangle. This can be verified using a protractor. Triangle 2 contains three acute angles, so it is classified as an acute triangle. Triangle 3 contains an obtuse angle, so it is an obtuse triangle.

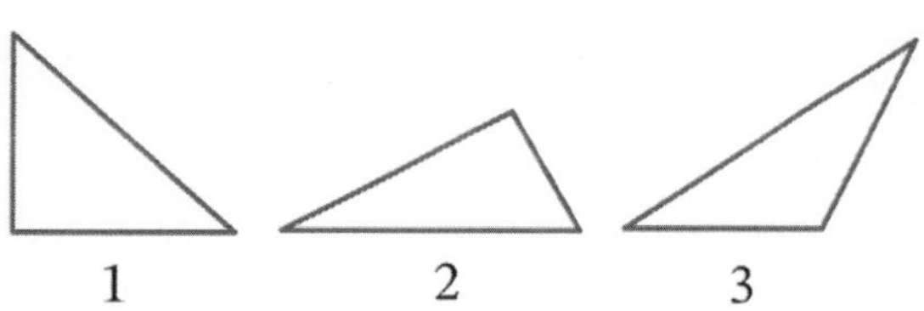

Parallel and Perpendicular Lines

When two lines are **parallel**, they **never intersect**. Parallel lines are like railroad tracks, extending side by side, but never crossing. **Perpendicular** lines **intersect** to form a **90-degree angle**. Perpendicular lines form **right angles**.

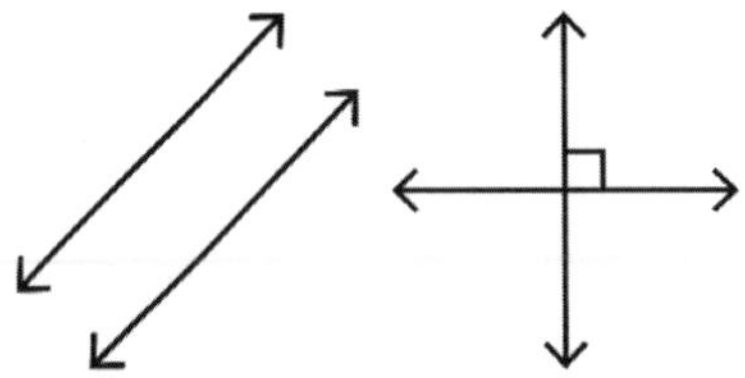

Two-dimensional figures can be classified based on their number of sides, their angle measures, and by the presence of parallel or perpendicular side lengths.

Polygons and Parallel and Perpendicular Lines

A **quadrilateral** is a four-sided shape. The table below shows 4 common quadrilaterals. Notice how trapezoids have exactly one pair of parallel sides, but parallelograms and rhombi have two pairs of parallel sides. Rectangles and squares have two pairs of parallel sides and four right angles formed by perpendicular side lengths.

	Exactly one pair of parallel sides	Trapezoid
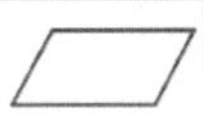	Two pairs of parallel sides	Parallelogram
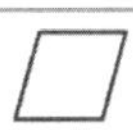	Parallelogram with congruent sides	Rhombus
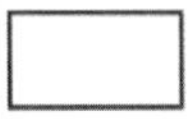	Parallelogram with right angles	Rectangle
	Rectangle with congruent sides	Square

Not all polygons will have parallel or perpendicular side lengths. For now, all of the shapes we talk about will have sides that are the same length, called **regular polygons**. Consider the regular polygons below. The triangle, pentagon, hexagon, heptagon, octagon, nonagon, and decagon have no right angles and no perpendicular sides. Some of the polygons do contain side lengths that are parallel. For example, the bottom side length and the top side length of a hexagon are parallel. Notice how the angle measures of the triangle are all acute, the angles in the quadrilateral are right, and the angle measures for all the other polygons are obtuse. When classifying two-dimensional shapes, it is important to look for characteristics such as parallel lines, perpendicular lines, acute angles, obtuse angles, and right angles.

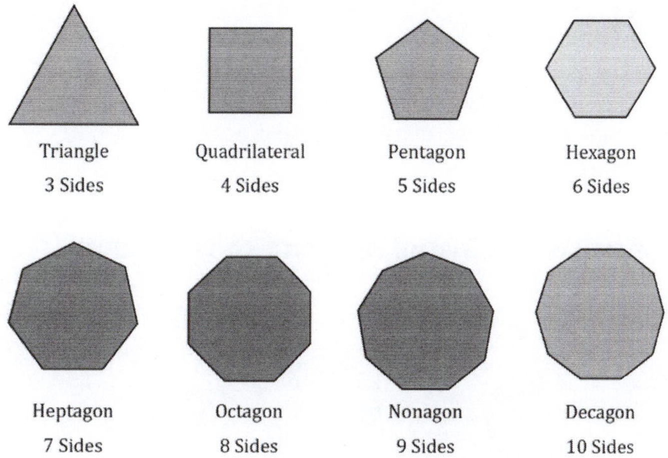

EXAMPLE

A quadrilateral with exactly one pair of parallel sides is classified as a ____________.

A trapezoid is defined as a four-sided shape with only one set of parallel sides.

EXAMPLE

Student A states that all squares are rectangles, but not all rectangles are squares. Student B states that all rectangles are squares, but not all squares are rectangles. Which student is correct?

All squares are rectangles, but not all rectangles are squares. The definition of a rectangle is a 4-sided figure with 4 right angles. A square qualifies as a rectangle because it has 4 sides and 4 right angles. However, a square has 4 equal sides. Not all rectangles have 4 equal sides, so not all rectangles are squares. Student A is correct.

Practice Test #1

1. Which of the following is largest?

a. 0.55
b. 0.500
c. 0.505
d. 0.0555

2. Which fraction is represented by the diagram shown below?

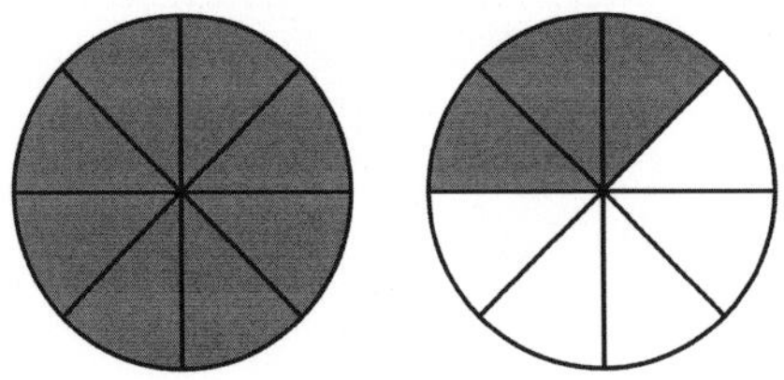

a. $1\frac{1}{8}$
b. $1\frac{1}{4}$
c. $1\frac{3}{8}$
d. $1\frac{1}{2}$

3. Which of the following models represents a fraction equivalent to $\frac{2}{5}$?

a.
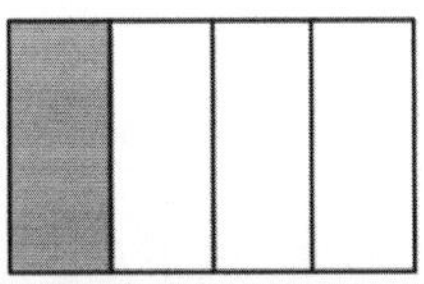

b.
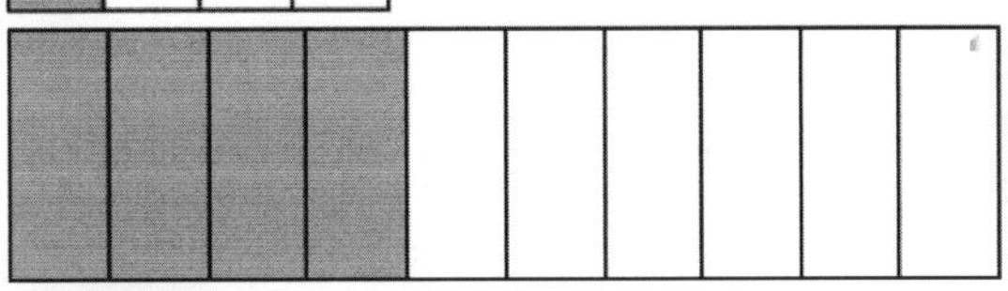

c.
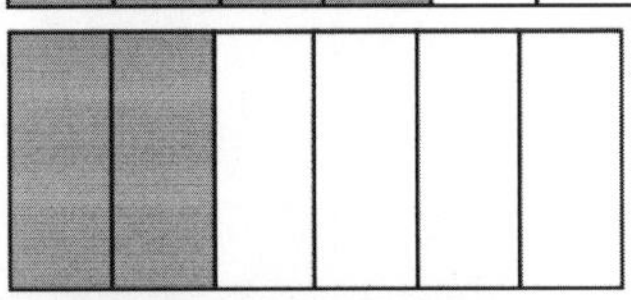

d.
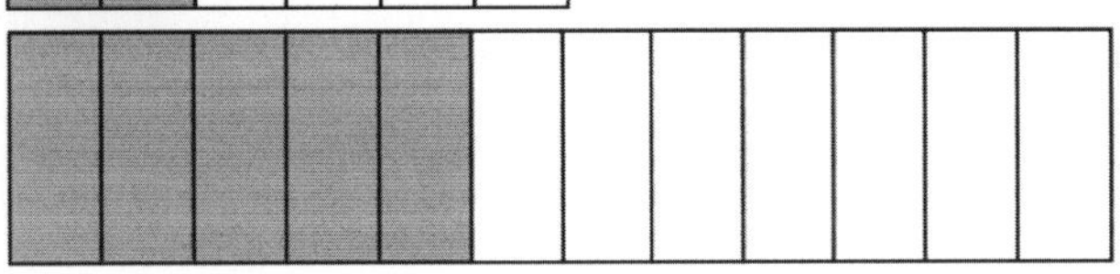

4. If Hannah drives 1104 miles a month and Carrie drives 1339 miles a month. How many miles do they drive each month combined?

a. 2443
b. 2445
c. 2475
d. 2433

5. Jasper collects 1,082 cans of food. He gives a certain number of cans to the first local charity he finds. He now has 602 cans of food. How many cans of food did he give to the first local charity?

a. 430
b. 480
c. 682
d. 1,684

6. Which shape has 4 congruent sides and 4 right angles?

a. square
b. rhombus
c. parallelogram
d. rectangle

7. Amanda creates the base of a picture frame, using 4.55 inches of red fabric and 6.25 inches of blue fabric. How many inches of fabric are used to create the base of the frame?

a. 10.80 inches
b. 10.85 inches
c. 10.75 inches
d. 10.90 inches

8. Travis has a stick that is 5/16 of a meter long, and Steven has a stick that is 7/8 of a meter long. If they lay the sticks end to end how long would they be?

a. $\frac{12}{16}$ meter
b. $1\frac{3}{16}$
c. $1\frac{3}{8}$
d. $1\frac{1}{8}$

9. Jenny will be in a parade and will be throwing out candy. She has 30 pieces of candy, but she thinks that she will need 8 times that much since the parade is so long. How many pieces does she think she needs?

a. 180
b. 240
c. 320
d. 210

10. If John works 386 minutes a day, how many minutes does he work in a 5 day work week?

a. 1935
b. 1500
c. 1900
d. 1930

11. Hannah ran 12 laps every day for 8 days. How many laps did she run in all?

a. 108
b. 96
c. 84
d. 72

12. Kevin approved 13 trees out of every group of trees he surveyed. He surveyed 15 groups of trees. How many trees did he approve?

a. 155
b. 165
c. 195
d. 205

13. Monique has $690 to spend on a 3-day trip. She plans to spend an equal amount of money per day. How many dollars can she spend per day?

a. 320
b. 2,070
c. 345
d. 230

14. Which of the following is the most reasonable estimate for the weight of a chair?

a. 1 ton
b. 15 pounds
c. 3 kilograms
d. 6 grams

15. Lynn has $316 to spend on groceries for the month. He plans to spend the same amount of money on groceries each week. How much money he can spend on groceries each week?

a. $65
b. $79
c. $90
d. $95

16. Carlisle charges $21.95 per haircut and has completed 30 haircuts this week. Which of the following is the best approximation for the total charges for all haircuts?

a. $450
b. $600
c. $750
d. $800

17. Which of the following number sentences belongs in the fact family shown below?

$$7 \times 6 = 42$$
$$6 \times 7 = 42$$
$$42 \div 7 = 6$$

a. $7 + 6 = 13$
b. $42 \div 6 = 7$
c. $42 + 7 = 49$
d. $42 - 6 = 36$

18. Billy is going on vacation. He will travel a total of 1486 miles while he is gone. If Location A is 572 miles away from home and then Location B is 437 miles from location A. How long is the trip from Location B back to home?

a. 477
b. 323
c. 1009
d. 523

19. A door is $7\frac{1}{4}$ feet tall. How many inches is it?

a. 84 inches
b. 90 inches
c. $84\frac{1}{4}$ inches
d. 87 inches

20. Choose the answers that make the statement correct.

The number 5,504 has two 5s. The 5 on the right is	_______ times	________ than the 5 on the left.
	1,000	smaller
	10	larger
	100	

21. Part A: The number of sit-ups Aisha has completed over a period of 3 days is shown in the table below.

Day, d	Number of Sit-ups, s
1	35
2	70
3	105

If this pattern continues, how many sit-ups will she have completed after 7 days?

a. 210
b. 280
c. 175
d. 245

Part B: What rule is used in the pattern above?

a. $d = 35 + s$
b. $s = 35d$
c. $s = 35 + d$
d. $d = 35s$

22. A sandbox has a length of 7.2 feet and a width of 3.98 feet. Which of the following best estimates the area of the sandbox?

a. 21 in^2
b. 32 in^2
c. 28 in^2
d. 24 in^2

23. If the measure of angle *BAC* is 38° and the measure of angle *DAE* is 49°, then what is the measure of angle *CAD*?

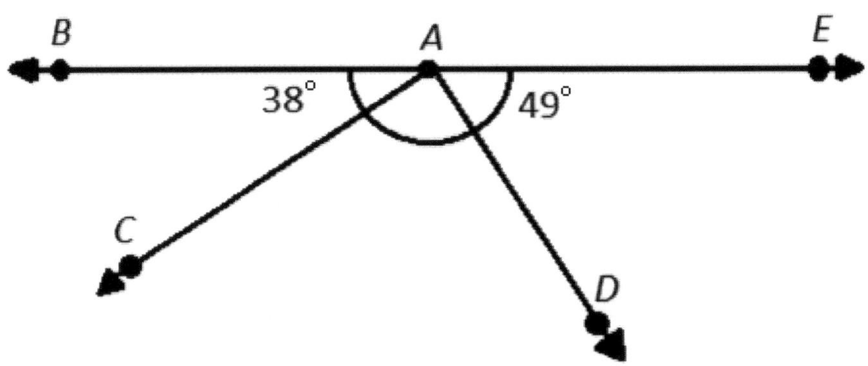

a. 177°
b. 87°
c. 93°
d. 52°

24. Choose the answers that make the statement correct.

When 286 is rounded to the nearest	_________	it becomes	____.
	ten		300
	hundred		280
			285

25. Which shape has 5 sides?

a. hexagon
b. pentagon
c. octagon
d. heptagon

26. Which symbol makes the following statement true?

348,762 ________ 349,761

a. <
b. >
c. =
d. None of the above.

27. Express the fraction $\frac{9}{100}$ as a decimal.

a. 0.9
b. 9.0
c. 0.09
d. 9.09

28. Which pair of fractions are equivalent?

a. $\frac{3}{4}$ and $\frac{6}{8}$
b. $\frac{3}{4}$ and $\frac{4}{8}$
c. $\frac{1}{4}$ and $\frac{1}{8}$
d. $\frac{3}{6}$ and $\frac{6}{8}$

29. Which word can be used to describe the triangle below?

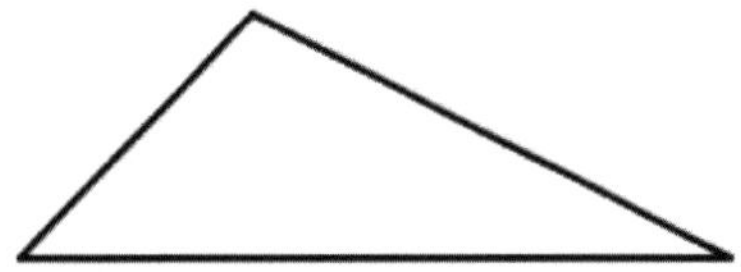

a. Equilateral
b. Scalene
c. Right
d. Obtuse

30. Which symbol best fits to complete the number sentence below?

$$\frac{12}{20} \underline{\qquad\qquad} \frac{1}{5}$$

a. >
b. <
c. =
d. None of the above.

31. The image below is a regular hexagon. How many lines of symmetry exist?

a. 0
b. 1
c. 2
d. 6

32. Ray *PX* is shown below. Another ray can be drawn from point *P* so that a 130° angle is formed. When starting at point *P*, which other point should the new ray pass through?

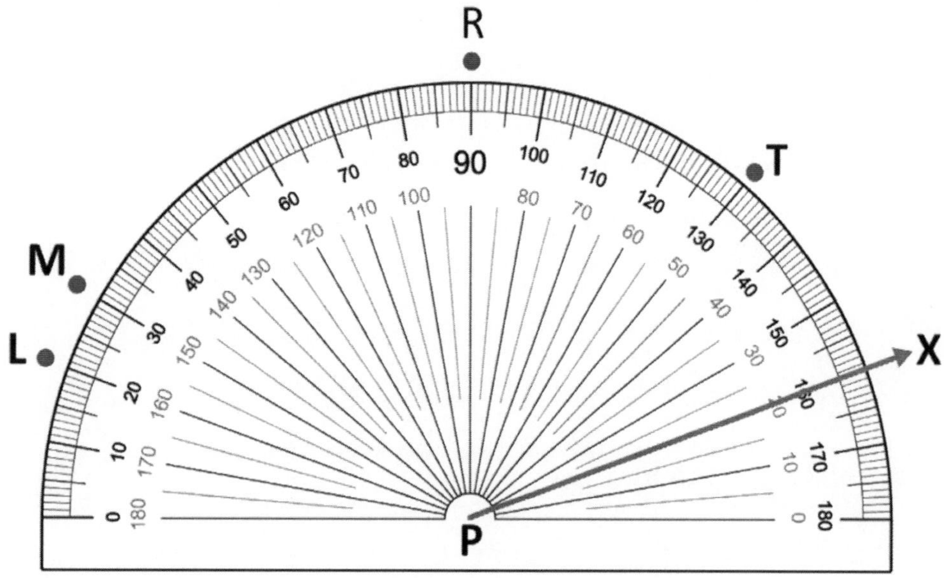

a. Point L
b. Point M
c. Point R
d. Point T

33. Choose the answers that make the statement correct.

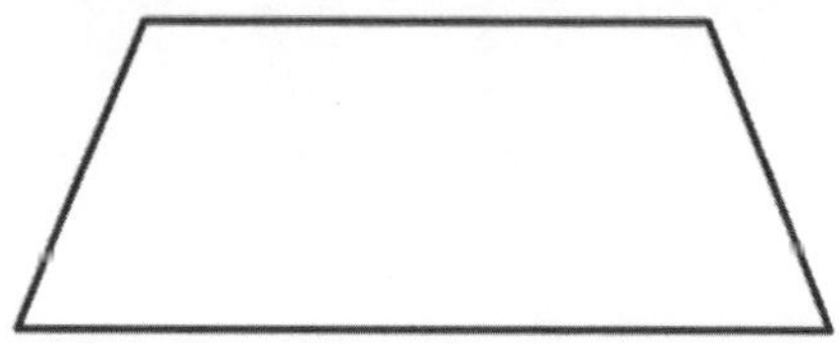

The shape above is called a ______________ and it has 1 ________________________.

parallelogram / rectangle / rhombus / trapezoid

right angle / pair of parallel sides / set of perpendicular sides

34. Which of the following are factors of 42?

a. 2 and 22
b. 3 and 14
c. 4 and 11
d. 5 and 8

35. Use the standard algorithm to divide 3,245 by 5.

a. 644
b. 649
c. 766
d. 934

36. Sally is making cupcakes. She needs $\frac{1}{4}$ cup of sugar for every 3 cupcakes. How many cups does she need for 24 cupcakes?

a. $1\frac{1}{2}$ cups
b. 8 cups
c. $\frac{3}{4}$ cup
d. 2 cups

37. Which fraction is equivalent to $\frac{7}{10}$?

a. $\frac{7}{100}$
b. $\frac{70}{100}$
c. $\frac{14}{100}$
d. $\frac{49}{100}$

38. Which of the following most accurately describes the pair of lines shown below?

a. Lines that do not intersect
b. Lines that intersect
c. Lines that do not intersect and remain the same distance apart
d. Lines that are perpendicular

39. The letter H exhibits symmetry with respect to a horizontal axis, as shown in the figure, as everything below the dashed line is a mirror image of everything above it. Which of the following letters does NOT exhibit horizontal symmetry?

a. C
b. D
c. Z
d. I

40. Which of the following represents perpendicular lines?

a.

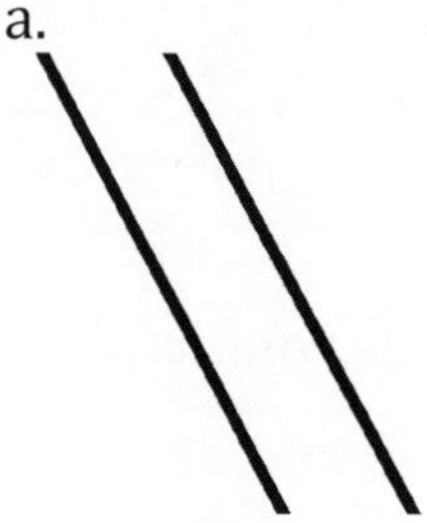

b.

c.

d.

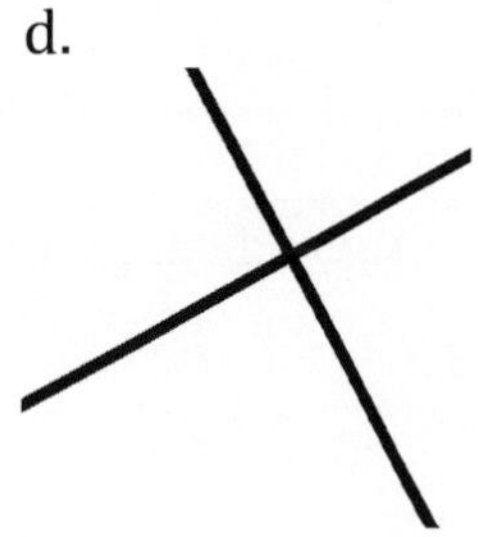

Answers and Explanations for Test #1

1. A: When comparing decimals, compare them one decimal place at a time. First compare the part before the decimal point; whichever has the largest whole part is largest. If the whole parts are equal, compare the tenths place, the place just after the decimal point. If the digits in the tenths place are the same, compare the hundredths place, the second place after the decimal point, and so on. In this case, all the decimals have a zero before the decimal point, so we'll start by comparing the tenths place. 0.55, 0.500, and 0.505 all have a 5 in the tenths place, while 0.0555 has a zero in the tenths place. So, 0.55, 0.500, and 0.505 are larger than 0.0555. Now, compare the hundredths place of the remaining choices, discarding the 0.0555 that we now know is smallest. 0.55 has a 5 in the hundredths place, while 0.500 and 0.505 both have zeroes. So, 0.55 is the largest of the choices.

2. C: The diagram represents one whole, plus three-eighths of a second whole. Therefore, the diagram represents the fraction, $1\frac{3}{8}$.

3. B: The fraction, $\frac{2}{5}$, is equivalent to the fraction, $\frac{4}{10}$. The numerator and denominator of the given fraction are both multiplied by 2 to obtain the model for $\frac{4}{10}$; the fractions are proportional.

4. A: To find their combined miles just add them together.

5. B: In order to find the number of cans of food he gave to the first charity, the number of cans of food he has left needs to be subtracted from the number of cans he collected; $1{,}082 - 602 = 480$.

6. A: A square has four congruent sides and four right angles. A rhombus has four congruent sides, but is not required to have four right angles.

7. A: The sum of the two decimals is 10.80; the decimals are added just like whole numbers are, while aligning the decimal point.

8. B: If they lay the sticks end to end then you would just add the lengths together. First convert $\frac{7}{8}$ to $\frac{14}{16}$ then add that to $\frac{5}{16}$ to get $1\frac{3}{16}$.

9. B: Jenny thinks she will need 240 pieces of candy for the parade since $30 \times 8 = 240$.

10. D: To find the answer multiply 386 times 5.

11. B: She runs 12×8 laps in all, or 96 laps.

12. C: Since he approved 13 trees out of every group of trees and surveyed 15 groups, he approved 13×15 trees, or 195 trees.

13. D: In order to find the amount of money she can spend each day, 690 should be divided by 3; $690 \div 3 = 230$. Thus, she can spend 230 dollars per day.

14. B: A chair may possibly weigh 15 pounds; 1 ton is equal to 2,000 pounds; 3 kilograms is equal to 3,000 grams; and 6 grams is the weight of about 12 pencils.

15. B: The amount of money Lynn has available to spend on groceries during each week of the month can be determined through division. There are four full weeks in a month, so $316 \div 4 = 79$.

16. B: The amount of money Carlisle charges per hair cut can be rounded to \$20; $20 \times 30 = 600$. Thus, his total charges are approximately \$600.

17. B: The missing number sentence in the fact family is the other division number sentence, which reads:$42 \div 6 = 7$.

18. A: If he travels 572 miles and then 437 miles then he only has 477 miles left to go. 1486-572-437=477.

19. D: There are 12 inches in a foot. $12 \times 7 = 84$. Then divide 12 by 4 to get 3. 84+3=87.

20. 10, smaller: The 5 on the left is in the thousands place, so it represents 5,000. The 5 on the right is in the hundreds place, so it represents 500. 5,000 is 10 times larger than 500. This can be checked with multiplication, $500 \times 10 = 5{,}000$. Every place value is 10 times larger than the place value to its right. Also, every place value is 10 times smaller than the place value to its left.

21. Part A: D. Since she completes 35 each day, she has completed 35×7 situps after 7 days; $35 \times 7 = 245$.

Part B: B: The number of days, *d*, is multiplied by 35 sit ups to find the total number of sit ups Aisha completes over the given period, *s*. Therefore, the rule is $s = 35d$.

22. C: The measurements of the sandbox can be rounded to 7 feet and 4 feet. The area of the sandbox is equal to the product of the measurements of the length and width of the box. Thus, the area is approximately 7×4, or 28 squared inches.

23. C: Since the angle of a straight line is known to be 180°, then $38°\ and\ 49°$can be subtracted from that to get 93°.

24. hundred, 300: On a number line, 286 is between 200 and 300. To round to the nearest hundred, look at the tens place. 8 is greater than or equal to 5, so the hundreds digit rounds up to 3 and the digits after becomes 0s. Therefore, 286 becomes 300 when rounded to the nearest hundred.

25. B: A pentagon has 5 sides.

26. A: When comparing numbers, look at place value. Both numbers have digits up to the hundred thousands place. The values in each position are equal until the thousands place. 9 is greater than 8, so 349,761 is greater than 348,762. That means the symbols needs to open to the right. The statement will be read as 348,762 is less than 349,761.

27. C: The fraction $\frac{9}{100}$ represents 9 hundredths. As a decimal, this means 9 in the hundredths place. The decimal 0.09 represents the fraction $\frac{9}{100}$.

28. A: $\frac{3}{4}$ and $\frac{6}{8}$ are equivalent because they are the same distance from 0 on a number line.

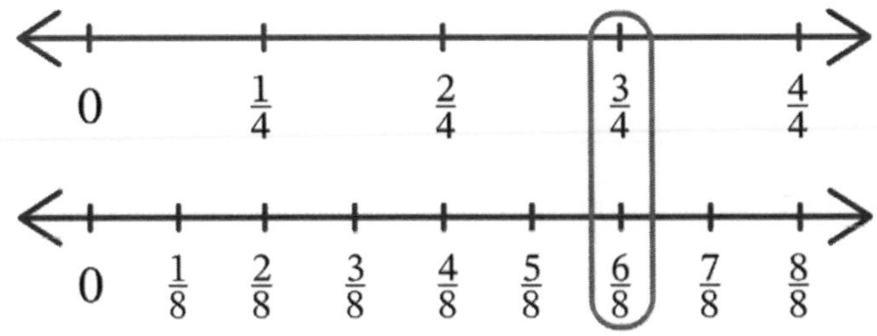

29. B: The triangle has no congruent side lengths, which means the triangle is classified as scalene.

30. A: One way to compare fractions is to put them both in simplest form. $\frac{1}{5}$ is already in simplest form. In the fraction $\frac{12}{20}$, the numerator and the denominator both share a greatest common factor of 4. Since $12 \div 4 = 3$ and $20 \div 4 = 5$, the simplest form of this fraction is $\frac{3}{5}$. Since $\frac{1}{5}$ and $\frac{3}{5}$ have a common denominator, it is easy to compare the fractions. The fraction with the greatest numerator is also the fraction with the greatest value. Thus, $\frac{3}{5}$ or $\frac{12}{20}$ is greater than $\frac{1}{5}$.

31. D: A regular hexagon has 6 lines of symmetry.

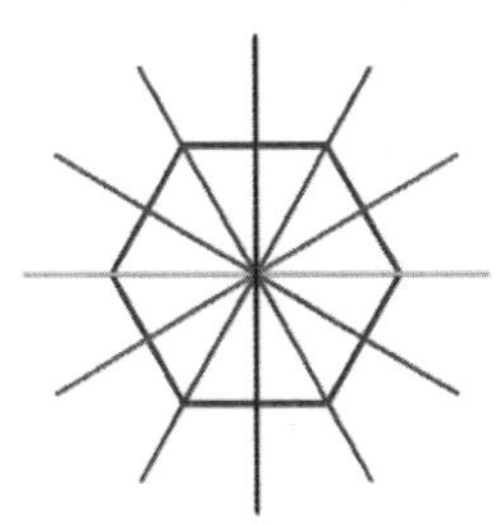

32. B: When a ray is constructed from point P to point M, an obtuse angle is formed. $\overrightarrow{PX}$ passes through the 160° mark on the outer edge of the protractor, and $\overrightarrow{PM}$ passes through the 30° mark on the outer edge of the protractor. To find the angle measure between these two rays, subtract the two values: $160° - 30° = 130°$. Therefore, $\angle XPM$ is a 130° angle.

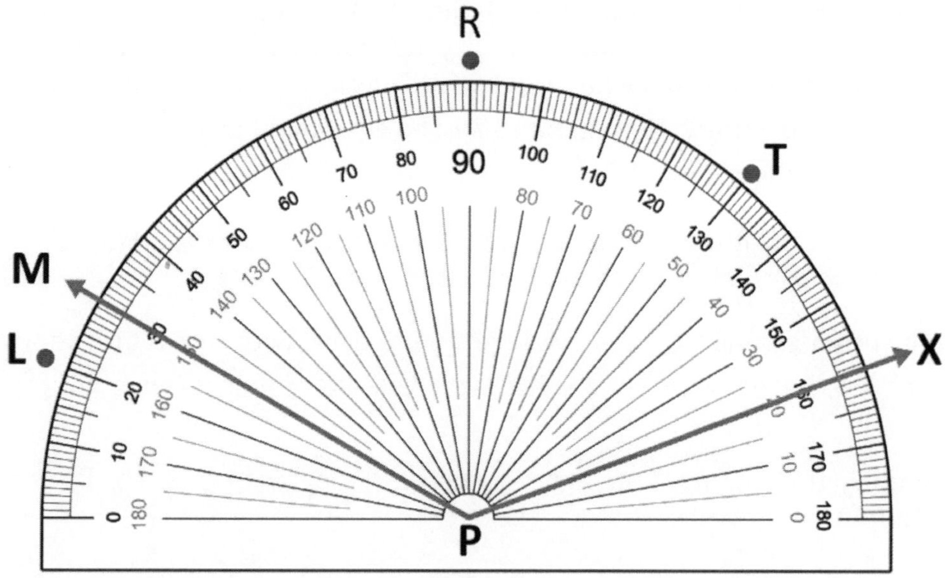

33. trapezoid, pair of parallel sides: This shape has one pair of parallel sides. A trapezoid has 4 sides, and exactly one pair of parallel sides. The shape is not a parallelogram, rectangle, or rhombus because those shapes have 2 pairs of parallel sides.

34. B: Factors are numbers that are multiplied together. Therefore, the only factors listed that would have a product of 42 is 3 and 14, since $3 \times 14 = 42$.

35. B: Use the standard algorithm. Follow the 4-step process:

1. Multiply
2. Subtract
3. Bring down
4. Repeat

5 goes into 32 six times, so write a 6 in the first spot of the answer. $6 \times 5 = 30$, so write this below 32. $32 - 30 = 2$. Bring down the 4. Repeat the cycle.

$$\begin{array}{r} 649 \\ 5\overline{)3245} \\ -\underline{30} \\ 24 \\ -\underline{20} \\ 45 \\ -\underline{45} \\ 0 \end{array}$$

36. D: If she needs to make 24 cupcakes and she knows the amount of sugar for 3 cupcakes then she just needs to multiply by 8. So $\frac{1}{4} \times 8 = \frac{8}{4} = 2$.

37. B: To determine equivalent fractions, the numerator and denominator need to share a common factor. Since $\frac{7}{10}$ is in simplest form, the numerator and denominator simply need to be multiplied by the same factor in order to determine an equivalent fraction. Since all of the denominators in the answer choices are 100, the factor can be determined by dividing 100 by 10. This results in 10, so the factor was 10. Thus, the numerator also needs to be multiplied by 10. Since 7 times 10 is equal to 70, the equivalent fraction is $\frac{70}{100}$.

38. C: The lines are parallel and do not intersect. However, the most accurate description includes the fact that the lines remain the same distance apart. Note. Lines may not intersect and not be parallel.

39.C: All of the other capital letters shown are symmetrical with respect to a horizontal axis drawn through the middle, as in the H shown in the figure. Only Z is not symmetrical in this respect

40. D: Perpendicular lines form four right angles, or 90 degree angles. The lines shown for Choice D form four right angles.

Practice Test #2

1. A room has 6 rows of 9 chairs. The room next to it has 32 chairs. Together how many chairs do they have?

a. 54
b. 56
c. 86
d. 84

2. A farm has only cows and chickens. There are 5 chicken coops with 14 chickens each, and 6 barns with 16 cows each. How many total animals are on the farm?

a. 41
b. 330
c. 164
d. 166

3. Which of the following sets represents a fraction equivalent to $\frac{8}{12}$?

a.

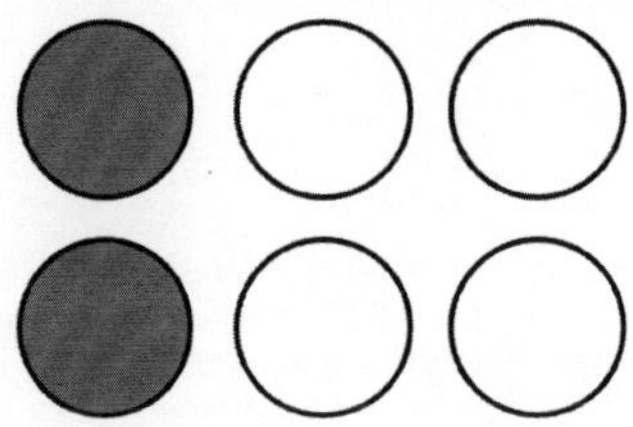

b.

c.

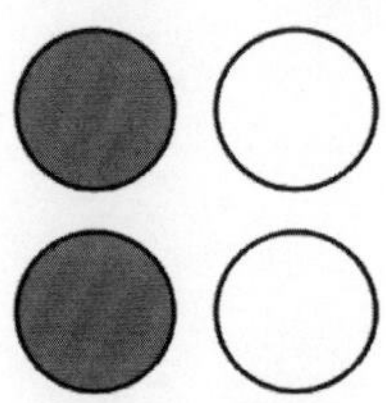

d.

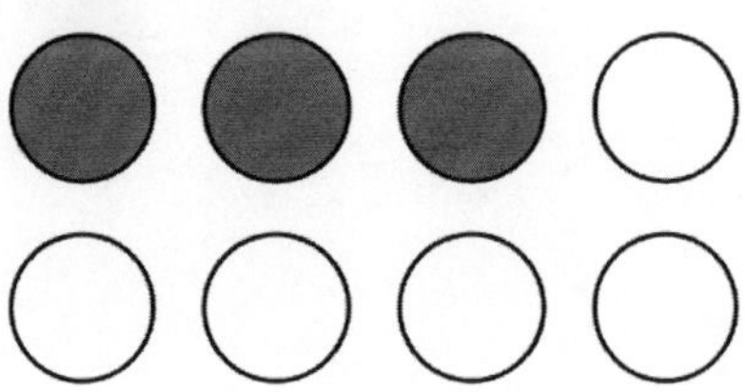

4. Which fraction is represented by the diagram shown below?

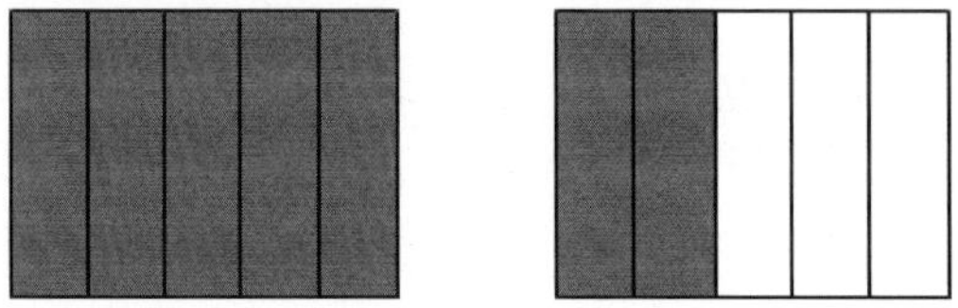

a. $1\frac{1}{2}$
b. $1\frac{2}{5}$
c. $1\frac{3}{5}$
d. $1\frac{3}{4}$

5. Which of the following models represents a fraction equal to the fraction shown below?

a. 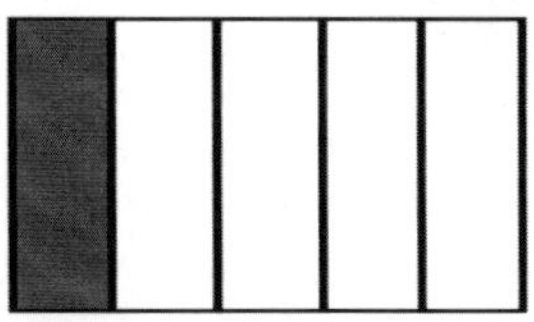

b. 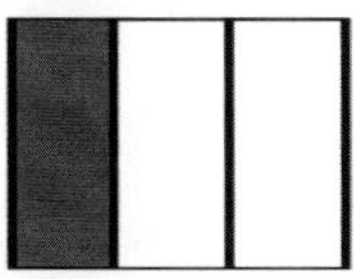

c. 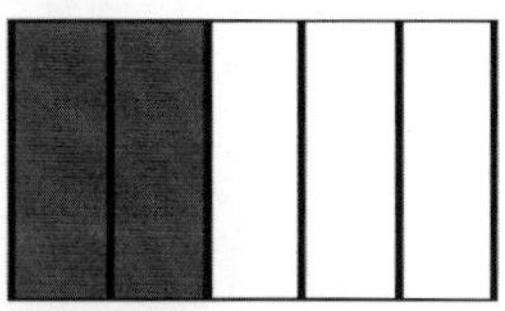

d. 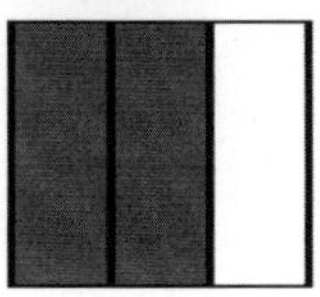

6. Which of the following fractions are equal to $\frac{2}{3}$?

a. $\frac{1}{6}$
b. $\frac{6}{9}$
c. $\frac{5}{8}$
d. $\frac{6}{10}$

7. Choose from the options below and write the correct answers in the blanks.

A 1 in the ten thousands place is ____________ than a 1 in the tens place.

100 smaller
1,000 larger

8. Andrea pays $120 more in rent per month this year than she did last year. She pays $763 per month this year. How much did she pay per month last year?

a. $663
b. $643
c. $863
d. $883

9. Which decimal is represented by the fractional value shown below?

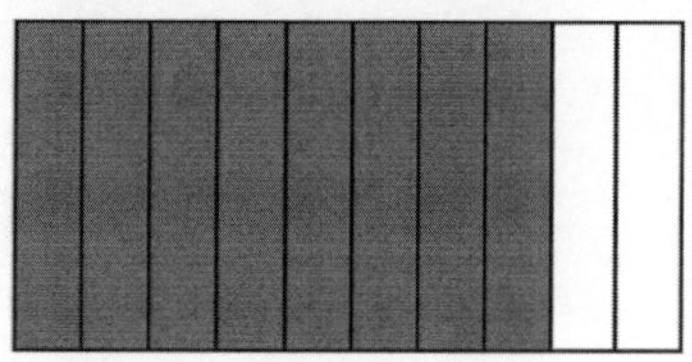

a. 0.08
b. 0.2
c. 0.10
d. 0.8

10. What is the 11th number in the pattern shown below?

10, 20, 30, 40, ...

a. 90
b. 100
c. 110
d. 120

11. Which of the following is the most reasonable estimate for the length of a book?

a. $\frac{1}{2}$ meter
b. $11\frac{1}{2}$ inches
c. 8 millimeters
d. 2 yards

12. Alex buys 3 gallons of milk each week. How many gallons of milk does he buy in 12 weeks?

a. 18
b. 24
c. 36
d. 48

13. A candle-making shop sold 18 candles on Friday, 37 candles on Saturday, and 23 candles on Sunday. Which of the following is the number of candles sold during the three days?

a. 68
b. 78
c. 87
d. 88

14. Jason walks 2,847 feet to school. Kevin walks 3,128 feet to school. What is the difference in the distance that they walk to school?

a. 5,975
b. 281
c. 1,721
d. 381

15. Which of the following shapes has four sides and only one set of parallel sides?

a. square
b. parallelogram
c. trapezoid
d. rectangle

16. Mr. Jacobsen buys 32 boxes of oatmeal. Each box contains 8 packets of oatmeal. How many total packets of oatmeal did he buy?

a. 4
b. 40
c. 120
d. 256

17. Mr. Johnson ordered 1 pizza for every 3 kids in his class. If he ordered 7 pizzas then how many kids does he have in his class?

a. 21
b. 14
c. 24
d. 10

18. Mr. Jacobsen writes the number sentences shown below:

$8 \times 9 = 72$
$9 \times 8 = 72$
$72 \div 9 = 8$

What is the fourth number sentence of this fact family?

a. $8 + 9 = 17$
b. $72 - 8 = 64$
c. $72 \div 8 = 9$
d. $17 - 9 = 8$

19. The number of miles Brad has driven over a period of 3 days is shown in the table below.

Day	Number of Miles
1	275
2	550
3	825

If this pattern continues, how many miles will he have driven after 8 days?

a. 2,000
b. 2,025
c. 2,075
d. 2,200

20. Ana draws a line with chalk that is $14\frac{5}{8}$ feet long. Then she erases $3\frac{3}{8}$ feet. How long is the line now?

a. $11\frac{1}{4}$
b. 12
c. $11\frac{1}{2}$
d. $10\frac{1}{4}$

21. $\angle ADB$ has a measure of 42°. $\angle BDC$ has a measure of 64°. What is the measure in degrees of $\angle ADC$?

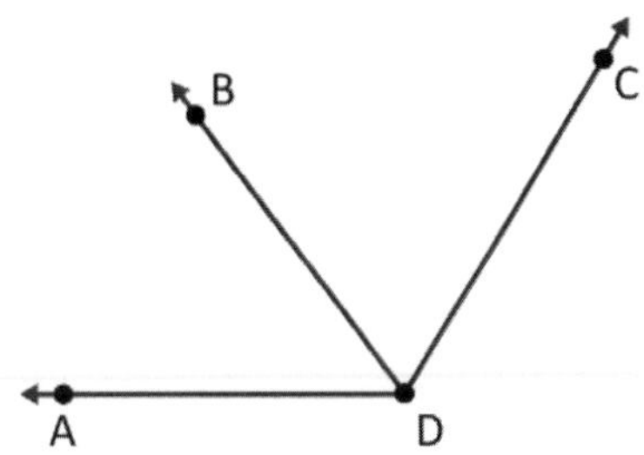

a. 106°
b. 116°
c. 96°
d. 126°

22. Which two names do NOT describe the shape? Select all that apply.

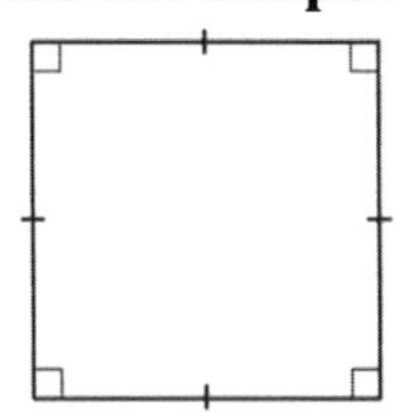

a. Square
b. Trapezoid
c. Parallelogram
d. Rhombus
e. Hexagon

23. When 751 is rounded to the nearest hundred it becomes ____.

a. 700
b. 750
c. 800
d. 760

24. Which fraction is equivalent to $\frac{3}{10}$?

a. $\frac{3}{100}$
b. $\frac{6}{100}$
c. $\frac{9}{100}$
d. $\frac{30}{100}$

25. Choose from the options below and write the correct answers in the blanks.

How many of the triangles below are considered right triangles?

___ of these triangles are considered right triangles because they each have ________________.

2	a right angle
3	three equal sides
4	an acute angle

26. Part A: Which of the following figures does not have any parallel sides?

a.

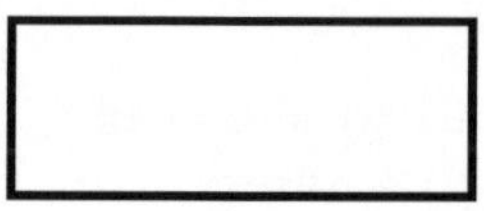

b.

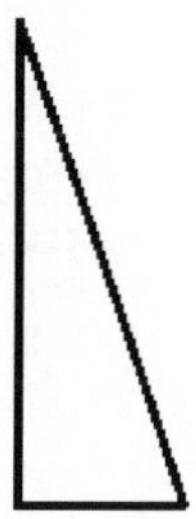

c.

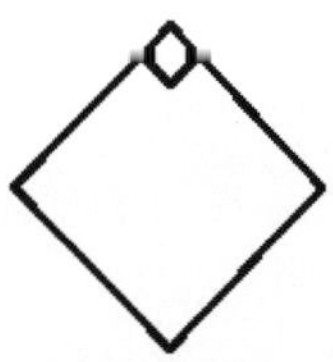

d.

Part B: What are parallel sides?

a. non-adjacent sides that maintain the same distance apart and will never intersect no matter how far the sides extend
b. sides that intersect at a 90° angle
c. adjacent sides that intersect at one point
d. non-adjacent sides that do not maintain the same distance apart and will eventually intersect if the sides are extended

27. The measure of the angle to the nearest degree is ___.

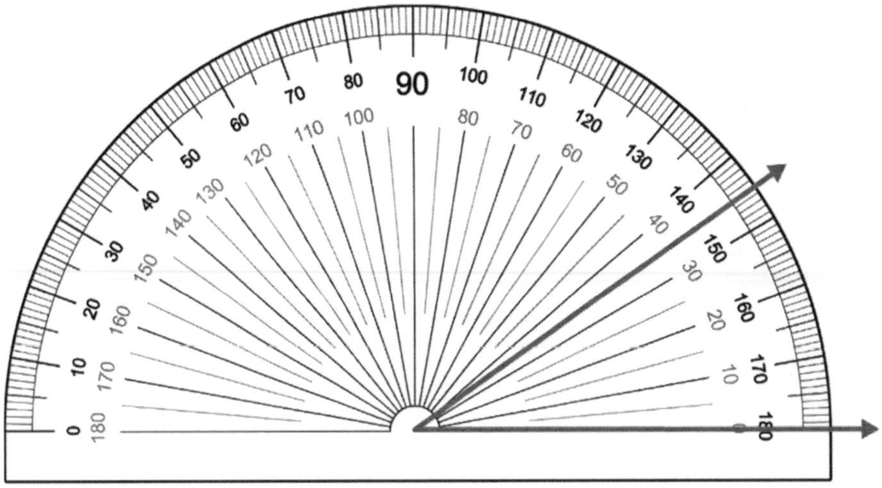

a. 145°
b. 45°
c. 135°
d. 35°

28. Isabelle must drive 1,482 miles. She plans to drive approximately the same number of miles per day over the period of 5 days. Which of the following is the best approximation for the number of miles she will drive per day?

a. 296
b. 336
c. 276
d. 286

29. Which symbol best fits to complete the number sentence below?

48.321 ________ 48.421

a. >
b. <
c. =
d. None of the above.

30. Pablo writes the number: 9,460,042. Which of the following represents this number, in words?

a. Nine hundred million, four hundred sixty thousand, forty-two
b. Nine million, four hundred sixty thousand, forty-two
c. Nine million, four hundred sixty, forty-two thousand
d. Nine, four hundred sixty, forty-two million thousand

31. Kay has 180 stickers. She divides the stickers equally among 8 children. Each child receives the same number of stickers. How many extra stickers will be remaining after Kay divides the stickers?

a. 2 stickers
b. 3 stickers
c. 4 stickers
d. 5 stickers

32. In the rectangle below each small square is one square unit. How many square units make up the area of the entire rectangle?

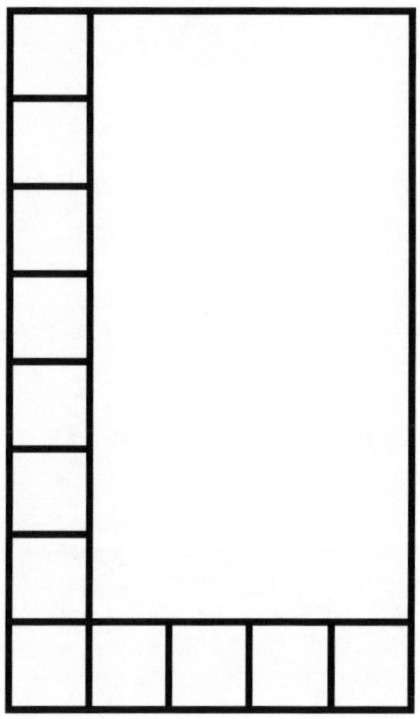

a. 28
b. 40
c. 12
d. 35

33. Hannah weighs approximately 27 pounds. What is her approximate weight, in ounces?

a. 432 ounces
b. 378 ounces
c. 324 ounces
d. 438 ounces

34. Jamal drinks 2 quarts of water per day. How many cups of water does he drink?

a. 16
b. 4
c. 8
d. 32

35. If Kara has 24 hair pins and she buys 6 more packages that each contain 12 hair pins. How many hair pins does she have now?

a. 72
b. 144
c. 96
d. 288

36. Define the polygon.

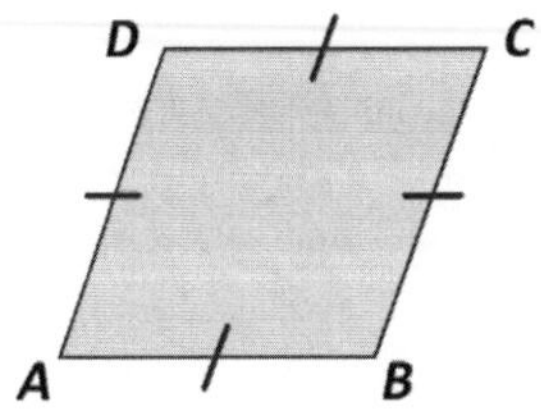

a. Square
b. Trapezoid
c. Pentagon
d. Rhombus

37. What is the correct name for the image below?

a. Line Segment
b. Line
c. Ray
d. Angle

38. Which of the following pairs of lines are parallel?

a.

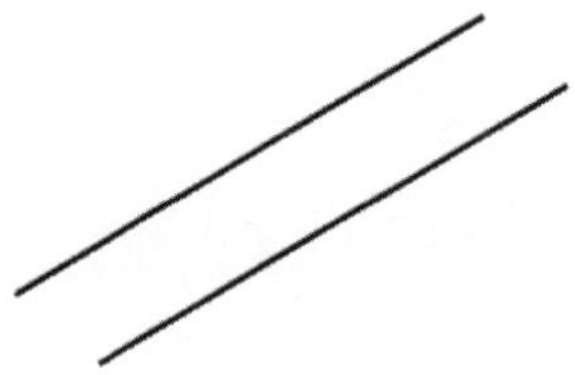

b.

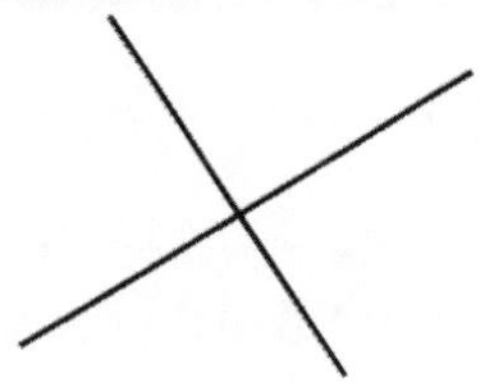

c.

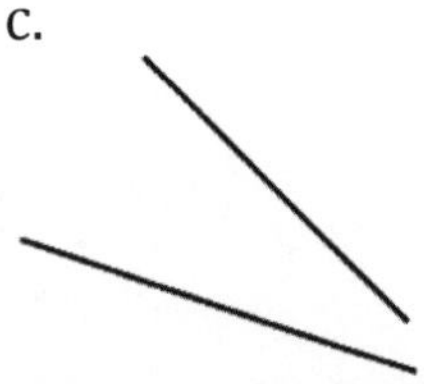

d.

39. Which symbol best fits to complete the number sentence below?

$\frac{14}{28}$ ______ $\frac{48}{50}$

a. >
b. <
c. =
d. None of the above.

40. Part A: Which of the following letter-shaped polygons has no line of symmetry?

a.

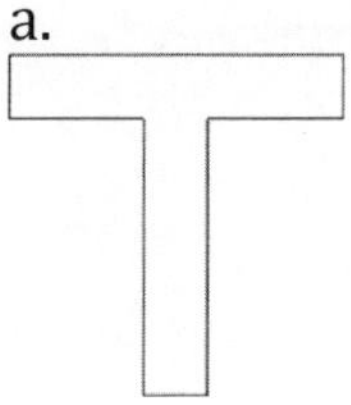

b.

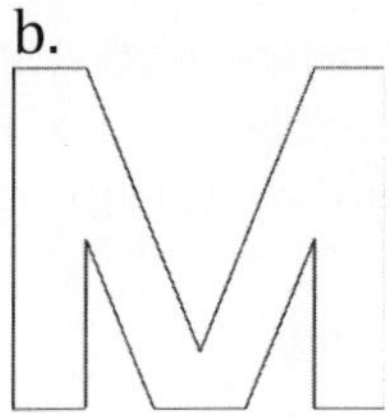

c.

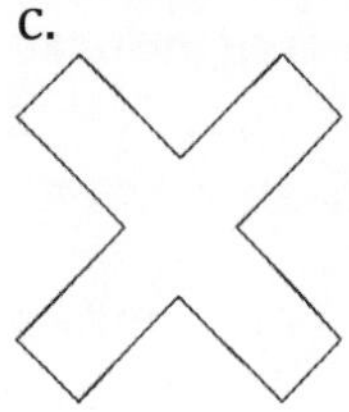

d.

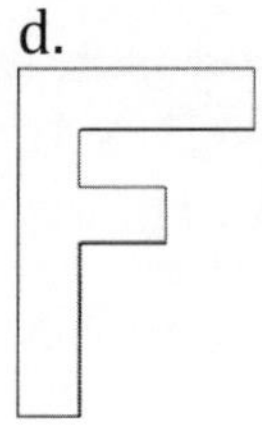

Part B: Which letter above has two lines of symmetry?

a. T
b. M
c. X
d. F

Answers and Explanations for Test #2

1. C: The first room contains, $6 \times 9 = 54$, chairs. The second contains 32. $54 + 32 = 86$.

2. D: Multiply the 5 chicken coops times the 14 chickens to get 70. Then multiply the 6 barns times the 16 cows to get 96. Add those together to get 166.

3. B: The fraction, $\frac{8}{12}$, is equivalent to the fraction, $\frac{2}{3}$. The numerator and denominator of the given fraction are both divided by 4 to obtain the model for $\frac{2}{3}$; the fractions are proportional.

4. B: The first diagram represents 1 whole, while the second diagram represents $\frac{2}{5}$. Thus, the diagram represents $1\frac{2}{5}$, in its entirety.

5. B: The fraction, $\frac{5}{15}$, is equivalent to the fraction, $\frac{1}{3}$. The numerator and denominator of the given fraction are both divided by 5 to obtain the model for $\frac{1}{3}$; the fractions are proportional.

6. B: $\frac{6}{9}$ can be reduced to $\frac{2}{3}$. This means the fractions are equivalent.

7. 1,000, larger: The 1 in the ten-thousands place represents 1 group of ten thousand, or 10,000. The 1 in the tens place represents 1 group of ten, or 10. 10,000 is 1,000 times larger than 10. To confirm this, multiply: $10 \times 1{,}000 = 10{,}000$.

8. B: Since Andrea paid $120 per month more last year, the amount she paid per month last year is equal to the difference of $763 and $120, or $643.

9. D: The diagram represents the fractional value $\frac{8}{10}$. This is equivalent to 0.8 as a decimal. Answer choice A is wrong because it is equivalent to $\frac{8}{100}$, which is smaller in value.

10. C: The value of each number in the pattern is a multiple of 10. Therefore, the 11th number represents the value of the product of 11 and 10; $11 \times 10 = 110$.

11. B: The length of a book is possibly $11\frac{1}{2}$ inches; one-half of a meter is 50 centimeters, which would be almost 2 feet; 8 millimeters is less than 1 centimeter; and 2 yards is equal to 6 feet. None of the other measurements are likely for a book length.

12. C: Alex will be 3×12 gallons of milk in 12 weeks, or 36 gallons of milk.

13. B: The number of candles sold is $18 + 37 + 23$ candles, or 78 candles.

14. B: To find the difference just subtract. 3128-2847=281

15. C: A trapezoid has 4 sides and only one pair of parallel sides. A square, parallelogram, and rectangle all have two pairs of parallel sides.

16. D: Each box contains 8 packets, so that is the same as 32×8, which is 256.

17. A: If 1 pizza feeds 3 people then you can multiply 7 times 3 to figure out that 7 pizzas feeds 21 people.

18. C: The missing number sentence in the fact family is the other division number sentence, which reads: $72 \div 8 = 9$.

19. D: Brad drives 275 miles each day. Thus, the total number of miles driven, over a period of days, can be found by adding 275 miles to the number of total miles driven for each previous day. In other words, after 4 days, he drove 1,100 miles. After 5 days, he drove 1,375 miles. After 6 days, he drove 1,650 miles. After 7 days, he drove 1,925 miles. After 8 days, he drove 2,200 miles.

20. A: To find the length just subtract $3\frac{3}{8}$ from $14\frac{5}{8}$.

21. A: The measure of $\angle ADC$ can be determined by adding the measure of $\angle ADB$ to the measure of $\angle BDC$. $\angle ADB$ is 42° and $\angle BDC$ is 64°, so the sum of these two angles is $42° + 64° = 106°$. The measure of $\angle ADC$ is 106°.

22. B, E: The shape can be classified as a square, parallelogram and rhombus. A parallelogram has two pairs of parallel sides. A rhombus has two pairs of parallel sides and all four sides are the same length. A square has two pairs of parallel sides, all four sides are the same length, and it has four right angles. This shape cannot be classified as a trapezoid because it has more than one pair of parallel sides. This shape also cannot be classified as a hexagon because hexagons have 6 sides.

23. C: Locate the digit in the hundreds place. The number 751 has a 7 in the hundreds place. Now look to the digit to the right. If this digit is 5 or more, round up. If this digit is 4 or less, round down. In this case, the digit to the right of 7 is 5, so 751 rounds up to 800.

24. D: To determine equivalent fractions, the numerator and denominator need to share a common factor. Since $\frac{3}{10}$ is in simplest form, the numerator and denominator simply need to be multiplied by the same factor in order to determine an equivalent fraction. Since all of the denominators in the answer choices are 100, the factor can be determined by dividing 100 by 10. This results in 10, so the factor was 10. Thus, the numerator also needs to be multiplied by 10. Since 3 times 10 is equal to 30, the equivalent fraction is $\frac{30}{100}$.

25. 2, a right angle: A right triangle contains a 90° angle. A 90° angle can be thought of as a corner angle. Two triangles in the group, the second and third triangles have 90° corner angles. The second and the third triangles are right triangles.

26. Part A: B: A triangle does not have any parallel sides.

Part B: Parallel sides are non-adjacent sides that maintain the same distance apart and will never intersect no matter how far the sides extend.

27. D: The right interior row of numbers starts at 0°. Start at 0° and move counterclockwise to meet the other ray. The other ray passes through 35° on the interior row of numbers, so the angle measures 35°.

28. A: The distance Isabelle drives divided by 5 days is equal to 296 R2 miles driven per day. This is 296 $\frac{2}{5}$ which is approximately 296 miles per day.

29. B: When comparing decimals, compare them one decimal place at a time. First compare the part before the decimal point; whichever has the largest whole part is largest. If the whole parts are equal, compare the tenths place, the place just after the decimal point. If the digits in the tenths place are the same, compare the hundredths place, the second place after the decimal point, and so on. In this case, all the decimals have a 48 before the decimal point, so we'll start by comparing the tenths place. The tenths place in 48.321 is 3, but the tenths place in 48.421 is 2. Therefore, 48.421 is greater than 48.321 since 4 is greater than 3. The number sentence will be read as 48.321 is less than 48.421.

30. B: The number, 9,460,042 has a 9 in the millions place, a 4 in the hundred-thousands place, a 6 in the ten-thousands place, a 0 in the thousands place, a 0 in the hundreds place, a 4 in the tens place, and a 2 in the ones place. The 9 represents "Nine million". The 460 is written as "Four hundred sixty thousand." The 4 in the tens place and the 2 in the ones place represents, "Forty-two." Therefore, the number is read, "Nine million, four hundred sixty thousand, forty-two."

31. C: Each child will receive 22 stickers: $180 \div 8 = 22$ r 4. Since there is a remainder of 4, this means there will be 4 stickers left over. A visual model can also be used to help determine this.

32. B: 8 units make up the length and 5 units make up the width. Area is length times width, so $8 \times 5 = 40$.

33. A: There are 16 ounces in one pound. Thus, her approximate weight, in ounces, is equal to the product of 27 and 16; $27 \times 16 = 432$. She weighs approximately 432 ounces.

34. C: There are 2 cups in 1 pint and 2 pints in 1 quart. There are 4 pints in 2 quarts. Thus, there are 4×2, or 8 cups, in 2 quarts.

35. C: If she buys 6 packages of 12 then she buys, $6 \times 12 = 72$. She already had 24, so 72+24=96.

36. D: A rhombus is defined as a parallelogram with four congruent sides. The hash marks on each side length indicate that all four sides are congruent. Polygon *ABCD* is a rhombus.

37. C: A ray consists of one point, and a line extending out from that point. The line extends indefinitely, which is represented by the arrow.

38. A: Parallel lines are lines that do not intersect and are the same distance apart entirely.

39. B: One way to compare fractions is to put them both in simplest form. In the fraction $\frac{14}{28}$, the numerator and the denominator both share a greatest common factor of 14. Since $14 \div 14 = 1$ and $28 \div 14 = 2$, the simplest form of this fraction is $\frac{1}{2}$. In the fraction $\frac{48}{50}$, the numerator and the denominator both share a greatest common factor of 2. Since $48 \div 2 = 24$ and $50 \div 2 = 25$, the simplest form of this fraction is $\frac{24}{25}$. A model can be helpful to determine which value is more, but $\frac{24}{25}$ is obviously greater than one-half since it is almost a full whole. Thus, $\frac{24}{25}$ or $\frac{48}{50}$ is greater than $\frac{1}{2}$ or $\frac{14}{28}$.

40. Part A: D: The letter T has a vertical line of symmetry that divides the letter into mirror-image left and right sides, as do the letters M and X. X also has a horizontal line of symmetry that divides the letter into mirror-image top and bottom parts. However, examination of the letter F shows that it has no line of symmetry.

Part B: C: The letter X has a vertical line of symmetry and a horizontal line of symmetry.

How to Overcome Test Anxiety

Just the thought of taking a test is enough to make most people a little nervous. A test is an important event that can have a long-term impact on your future, so it's important to take it seriously and it's natural to feel anxious about performing well. But just because anxiety is normal, that doesn't mean that it's helpful in test taking, or that you should simply accept it as part of your life. Anxiety can have a variety of effects. These effects can be mild, like making you feel slightly nervous, or severe, like blocking your ability to focus or remember even a simple detail.

If you experience test anxiety—whether severe or mild—it's important to know how to beat it. To discover this, first you need to understand what causes test anxiety.

Causes of Test Anxiety

While we often think of anxiety as an uncontrollable emotional state, it can actually be caused by simple, practical things. One of the most common causes of test anxiety is that a person does not feel adequately prepared for their test. This feeling can be the result of many different issues such as poor study habits or lack of organization, but the most common culprit is time management. Starting to study too late, failing to organize your study time to cover all of the material, or being distracted while you study will mean that you're not well prepared for the test. This may lead to cramming the night before, which will cause you to be physically and mentally exhausted for the test. Poor time management also contributes to feelings of stress, fear, and hopelessness as you realize you are not well prepared but don't know what to do about it.

Other times, test anxiety is not related to your preparation for the test but comes from unresolved fear. This may be a past failure on a test, or poor performance on tests in general. It may come from comparing yourself to others who seem to be performing better or from the stress of living up to expectations. Anxiety may be driven by fears of the future—how failure on this test would affect your educational and career goals. These fears are often completely irrational, but they can still negatively impact your test performance.

Elements of Test Anxiety

As mentioned earlier, test anxiety is considered to be an emotional state, but it has physical and mental components as well. Sometimes you may not even realize that you are suffering from test anxiety until you notice the physical symptoms. These can include trembling hands, rapid heartbeat, sweating, nausea, and tense muscles. Extreme anxiety may lead to fainting or vomiting. Obviously, any of these symptoms can have a negative impact on testing. It is important to recognize them as soon as they begin to occur so that you can address the problem before it damages your performance.

The mental components of test anxiety include trouble focusing and inability to remember learned information. During a test, your mind is on high alert, which can help you recall information and stay focused for an extended period of time. However, anxiety interferes with your mind's natural processes, causing you to blank out, even on the questions you know well. The strain of testing during anxiety makes it difficult to stay focused, especially on a test that may take several hours. Extreme anxiety can take a huge mental toll, making it difficult not only to recall test information but even to understand the test questions or pull your thoughts together.

Effects of Test Anxiety

Test anxiety is like a disease—if left untreated, it will get progressively worse. Anxiety leads to poor performance, and this reinforces the feelings of fear and failure, which in turn lead to poor performances on subsequent tests. It can grow from a mild nervousness to a crippling condition. If allowed to progress, test anxiety can have a big impact on your schooling, and consequently on your future.

Test anxiety can spread to other parts of your life. Anxiety on tests can become anxiety in any stressful situation, and blanking on a test can turn into panicking in a job situation. But fortunately, you don't have to let anxiety rule your testing and determine your grades. There are a number of relatively simple steps you can take to move past anxiety and function normally on a test and in the rest of life.

Physical Steps for Beating Test Anxiety

While test anxiety is a serious problem, the good news is that it can be overcome. It doesn't have to control your ability to think and remember information. While it may take time, you can begin taking steps today to beat anxiety.

Just as your first hint that you may be struggling with anxiety comes from the physical symptoms, the first step to treating it is also physical. Rest is crucial for having a clear, strong mind. If you are tired, it is much easier to give in to anxiety. But if you establish good sleep habits, your body and mind will be ready to perform optimally, without the strain of exhaustion. Additionally, sleeping well helps you to retain information better, so you're more likely to recall the answers when you see the test questions.

Getting good sleep means more than going to bed on time. It's important to allow your brain time to relax. Take study breaks from time to time so it doesn't get overworked, and don't study right before bed. Take time to rest your mind before trying to rest your body, or you may find it difficult to fall asleep.

Along with sleep, other aspects of physical health are important in preparing for a test. Good nutrition is vital for good brain function. Sugary foods and drinks may give a burst of energy but this burst is followed by a crash, both physically and emotionally. Instead, fuel your body with protein and vitamin-rich foods.

Also, drink plenty of water. Dehydration can lead to headaches and exhaustion, especially if your brain is already under stress from the rigors of the test. Particularly if your test is a long one, drink water during the breaks. And if possible, take an energy-boosting snack to eat between sections.

Along with sleep and diet, a third important part of physical health is exercise. Maintaining a steady workout schedule is helpful, but even taking 5-minute study breaks to walk can help get your blood pumping faster and clear your head. Exercise also releases endorphins, which contribute to a positive feeling and can help combat test anxiety.

When you nurture your physical health, you are also contributing to your mental health. If your body is healthy, your mind is much more likely to be healthy as well. So take time to rest, nourish your body with healthy food and water, and get moving as much as possible. Taking these physical steps will make you stronger and more able to take the mental steps necessary to overcome test anxiety.

Mental Steps for Beating Test Anxiety

Working on the mental side of test anxiety can be more challenging, but as with the physical side, there are clear steps you can take to overcome it. As mentioned earlier, test anxiety often stems from lack of preparation, so the obvious solution is to prepare for the test. Effective studying may be the most important weapon you have for beating test anxiety, but you can and should employ several other mental tools to combat fear.

First, boost your confidence by reminding yourself of past success—tests or projects that you aced. If you're putting as much effort into preparing for this test as you did for those, there's no reason you should expect to fail here. Work hard to prepare; then trust your preparation.

Second, surround yourself with encouraging people. It can be helpful to find a study group, but be sure that the people you're around will encourage a positive attitude. If you spend time with others who are anxious or cynical, this will only contribute to your own anxiety. Look for others who are motivated to study hard from a desire to succeed, not from a fear of failure.

Third, reward yourself. A test is physically and mentally tiring, even without anxiety, and it can be helpful to have something to look forward to. Plan an activity following the test, regardless of the outcome, such as going to a movie or getting ice cream.

When you are taking the test, if you find yourself beginning to feel anxious, remind yourself that you know the material. Visualize successfully completing the test. Then take a few deep, relaxing breaths and return to it. Work through the questions carefully but with confidence, knowing that you are capable of succeeding.

Developing a healthy mental approach to test taking will also aid in other areas of life. Test anxiety affects more than just the actual test—it can be damaging to your mental health and even contribute to depression. It's important to beat test anxiety before it becomes a problem for more than testing.

Study Strategy

Being prepared for the test is necessary to combat anxiety, but what does being prepared look like? You may study for hours on end and still not feel prepared. What you need is a strategy for test prep. The next few pages outline our recommended steps to help you plan out and conquer the challenge of preparation.

Step 1: Scope Out the Test

Learn everything you can about the format (multiple choice, essay, etc.) and what will be on the test. Gather any study materials, course outlines, or sample exams that may be available. Not only will this help you to prepare, but knowing what to expect can help to alleviate test anxiety.

Step 2: Map Out the Material

Look through the textbook or study guide and make note of how many chapters or sections it has. Then divide these over the time you have. For example, if a book has 15 chapters and you have five days to study, you need to cover three chapters each day. Even better, if you have the time, leave an extra day at the end for overall review after you have gone through the material in depth.

If time is limited, you may need to prioritize the material. Look through it and make note of which sections you think you already have a good grasp on, and which need review. While you are studying, skim quickly through the familiar sections and take more time on the challenging parts. Write out your plan so you don't get lost as you go. Having a written plan also helps you feel more in control of the study, so anxiety is less likely to arise from feeling overwhelmed at the amount to cover.

Step 3: Gather Your Tools

Decide what study method works best for you. Do you prefer to highlight in the book as you study and then go back over the highlighted portions? Or do you type out notes of the important information? Or is it helpful to make flashcards that you can carry with you? Assemble the pens, index cards, highlighters, post-it notes, and any other materials you may need so you won't be distracted by getting up to find things while you study.

If you're having a hard time retaining the information or organizing your notes, experiment with different methods. For example, try color-coding by subject with colored pens, highlighters, or post-it notes. If you learn better by hearing, try recording yourself reading your notes so you can listen while in the car, working out, or simply sitting at your desk. Ask a friend to quiz you from your flashcards, or try teaching someone the material to solidify it in your mind.

Step 4: Create Your Environment

It's important to avoid distractions while you study. This includes both the obvious distractions like visitors and the subtle distractions like an uncomfortable chair (or a too-comfortable couch that makes you want to fall asleep). Set up the best study environment possible: good lighting and a comfortable work area. If background music helps you focus, you may want to turn it on, but otherwise keep the room quiet. If you are using a computer to take notes, be sure you don't have any other windows open, especially applications like social media, games, or anything else that could distract you. Silence your phone and turn off notifications. Be sure to keep water close by so you stay hydrated while you study (but avoid unhealthy drinks and snacks).

Also, take into account the best time of day to study. Are you freshest first thing in the morning? Try to set aside some time then to work through the material. Is your mind clearer in the afternoon or evening? Schedule your study session then. Another method is to study at the same time of day that you will take the test, so that your brain gets used to working on the material at that time and will be ready to focus at test time.

Step 5: Study!

Once you have done all the study preparation, it's time to settle into the actual studying. Sit down, take a few moments to settle your mind so you can focus, and begin to follow your study plan. Don't give in to distractions or let yourself procrastinate. This is your time to prepare so you'll be ready to fearlessly approach the test. Make the most of the time and stay focused.

Of course, you don't want to burn out. If you study too long you may find that you're not retaining the information very well. Take regular study breaks. For example, taking five minutes out of every hour to walk briskly, breathing deeply and swinging your arms, can help your mind stay fresh.

As you get to the end of each chapter or section, it's a good idea to do a quick review. Remind yourself of what you learned and work on any difficult parts. When you feel that you've mastered the material, move on to the next part. At the end of your study session, briefly skim through your notes again.

But while review is helpful, cramming last minute is NOT. If at all possible, work ahead so that you won't need to fit all your study into the last day. Cramming overloads your brain with more information than it can process and retain, and your tired mind may struggle to recall even previously learned information when it is overwhelmed with last-minute study. Also, the urgent nature of cramming and the stress placed on your brain contribute to anxiety. You'll be more likely to go to the test feeling unprepared and having trouble thinking clearly.

So don't cram, and don't stay up late before the test, even just to review your notes at a leisurely pace. Your brain needs rest more than it needs to go over the information again. In fact, plan to finish your studies by noon or early afternoon the day before the test. Give your brain the rest of the day to relax or focus on other things, and get a good night's sleep. Then you will be fresh for the test and better able to recall what you've studied.

Step 6: Take a Practice Test

Many courses offer sample tests, either online or in the study materials. This is an excellent resource to check whether you have mastered the material, as well as to prepare for the test format and environment.

Check the test format ahead of time: the number of questions, the type (multiple choice, free response, etc.), and the time limit. Then create a plan for working through them. For example, if you have 30 minutes to take a 60-question test, your limit is 30 seconds per question. Spend less time on the questions you know well so that you can take more time on the difficult ones.

If you have time to take several practice tests, take the first one open book, with no time limit. Work through the questions at your own pace and make sure you fully understand them. Gradually work up to taking a test under test conditions: sit at a desk with all study materials put away and set a timer. Pace yourself to make sure you finish the test with time to spare and go back to check your answers if you have time.

After each test, check your answers. On the questions you missed, be sure you understand why you missed them. Did you misread the question (tests can use tricky wording)? Did you forget the information? Or was it something you hadn't learned? Go back and study any shaky areas that the practice tests reveal.

Taking these tests not only helps with your grade, but also aids in combating test anxiety. If you're already used to the test conditions, you're less likely to worry about it, and working through tests until you're scoring well gives you a confidence boost. Go through the practice tests until you feel comfortable, and then you can go into the test knowing that you're ready for it.

Test Tips

On test day, you should be confident, knowing that you've prepared well and are ready to answer the questions. But aside from preparation, there are several test day strategies you can employ to maximize your performance.

First, as stated before, get a good night's sleep the night before the test (and for several nights before that, if possible). Go into the test with a fresh, alert mind rather than staying up late to study.

Try not to change too much about your normal routine on the day of the test. It's important to eat a nutritious breakfast, but if you normally don't eat breakfast at all, consider eating just a protein bar. If you're a coffee drinker, go ahead and have your normal coffee. Just make sure you time it so that the caffeine doesn't wear off right in the middle of your test. Avoid sugary beverages, and drink enough water to stay hydrated but not so much that you need a restroom break 10 minutes into the test. If your test isn't first thing in the morning, consider going for a walk or doing a light workout before the test to get your blood flowing.

Allow yourself enough time to get ready, and leave for the test with plenty of time to spare so you won't have the anxiety of scrambling to arrive in time. Another reason to be early is to select a good seat. It's helpful to sit away from doors and windows, which can be distracting. Find a good seat, get out your supplies, and settle your mind before the test begins.

When the test begins, start by going over the instructions carefully, even if you already know what to expect. Make sure you avoid any careless mistakes by following the directions.

Then begin working through the questions, pacing yourself as you've practiced. If you're not sure on an answer, don't spend too much time on it, and don't let it shake your confidence. Either skip it and come back later, or eliminate as many wrong answers as possible and guess among the remaining ones. Don't dwell on these questions as you continue—put them out of your mind and focus on what lies ahead.

Be sure to read all of the answer choices, even if you're sure the first one is the right answer. Sometimes you'll find a better one if you keep reading. But don't second-guess yourself if you do immediately know the answer. Your gut instinct is usually right. Don't let test anxiety rob you of the information you know.

If you have time at the end of the test (and if the test format allows), go back and review your answers. Be cautious about changing any, since your first instinct tends to be correct, but make sure you didn't misread any of the questions or accidentally mark the wrong answer choice. Look over any you skipped and make an educated guess.

At the end, leave the test feeling confident. You've done your best, so don't waste time worrying about your performance or wishing you could change anything. Instead, celebrate the successful completion of this test. And finally, use this test to learn how to deal with anxiety even better next time.

Review Video: Test Anxiety
Visit mometrix.com/academy and enter code: 100340

Important Qualification

Not all anxiety is created equal. If your test anxiety is causing major issues in your life beyond the classroom or testing center, or if you are experiencing troubling physical symptoms related to your anxiety, it may be a sign of a serious physiological or psychological condition. If this sounds like your situation, we strongly encourage you to seek professional help.

How to Overcome Your Fear of Math

Not again. You're sitting in math class, look down at your test, and immediately start to panic. Your stomach is in knots, your heart is racing, and you break out in a cold sweat. You're staring at the paper, but everything looks like it's written in a foreign language. Even though you studied, you're blanking out on how to begin solving these problems.

Does this sound familiar? If so, then you're not alone! You may be like millions of other people who experience math anxiety. Anxiety about performing well in math is a common experience for students of all ages. In this article, we'll discuss what math anxiety is, common misconceptions about learning math, and tips and strategies for overcoming math anxiety.

What Is Math Anxiety?

Psychologist Mark H. Ashcraft explains math anxiety as a feeling of tension, apprehension, or fear that interferes with math performance. Having math anxiety negatively impacts people's beliefs about themselves and what they can achieve. It hinders achievement within the math classroom and affects the successful application of mathematics in the real world.

Symptoms and Signs of Math Anxiety

To overcome math anxiety, you must recognize its symptoms. Becoming aware of the signs of math anxiety is the first step in addressing and resolving these fears.

Negative Self-Talk

If you have math anxiety, you've most likely said at least one of these statements to yourself:

- "I hate math."
- "I'm not good at math."
- "I'm not a math person."

The way we speak to ourselves and think about ourselves matters. Our thoughts become our words, our words become our actions, and our actions become our habits. Thinking negatively about math creates a self-fulfilling prophecy. In other words, if you take an idea as a fact, then it will come true because your behaviors will align to match it.

Avoidance

Some people who are fearful or anxious about math will tend to avoid it altogether. Avoidance can manifest in the following ways:

- Lack of engagement with math content
- Not completing homework and other assignments
- Not asking for help when needed

- Skipping class
- Avoiding math-related courses and activities

Avoidance is one of the most harmful impacts of math anxiety. If you steer clear of math at all costs, then you can't set yourself up for the success you deserve.

Lack of Motivation

Students with math anxiety may experience a lack of motivation. They may struggle to find the incentive to get engaged with what they view as a frightening subject. These students are often overwhelmed, making it difficult for them to complete or even start math assignments.

Procrastination

Another symptom of math anxiety is procrastination. Students may voluntarily delay or postpone their classwork and assignments, even if they know there will be a negative consequence for doing so. Additionally, they may choose to wait until the last minute to start projects and homework, even when they know they need more time to put forth their best effort.

Physiological Reactions

Many people with a fear of math experience physiological side effects. These may include an increase in heart rate, sweatiness, shakiness, nausea, and irregular breathing. These symptoms make it difficult to focus on the math content, causing the student even more stress and fear.

Strong Emotional Responses

Math anxiety also affects people on an emotional level. Responding to math content with strong emotions such as panic, anger, or despair can be a sign of math anxiety.

Low Test Scores and Performance

Low achievement can be both a symptom and a cause of math anxiety. When someone does not take the steps needed to perform well on tests and assessments, they are less likely to pass. The more they perform poorly, the more they accept this poor performance as a fact that can't be changed.

Feeling Alone

People who experience math anxiety feel like they are the only ones struggling, even if the math they are working on is challenging to many people. Feeling isolated in what they perceive as failure can trigger tension or nervousness.

Feeling of Permanency

Math anxiety can feel very permanent. You may assume that you are naturally bad at math and always will be. Viewing math as a natural ability rather than a skill that can be learned causes people to believe that nothing will help them improve. They take their current math abilities as fact and assume that they can't be changed. As a result, they give up, stop trying to improve, and avoid engaging with math altogether.

Lack of Confidence

People with low self-confidence in math tend to feel awkward and incompetent when asked to solve a math problem. They don't feel comfortable taking chances or risks when problem-solving because they second-guess themselves and assume they are incorrect. They don't trust in their ability to learn the content and solve problems correctly.

Panic

A general sense of unexplained panic is also a sign of math anxiety. You may feel a sudden sense of fear that triggers physical reactions, even when there is no apparent reason for such a response.

Causes Of Math Anxiety

Math anxiety can start at a young age and may have one or more underlying causes. Common causes of math anxiety include the following:

The Attitude of Parents or Guardians

Parents often put pressure on their children to perform well in school. Although their intentions are usually good, this pressure can lead to anxiety, especially if the student is struggling with a subject or class.

Perhaps your parents or others in your life hold negative predispositions about math based on their own experiences. For instance, if your mother once claimed she was not good at math, then you might have incorrectly interpreted this as a predisposed trait that was passed down to you.

Teacher Influence

Students often pick up on their teachers' attitudes about the content being taught. If a teacher is happy and excited about math, students are more likely to mirror these emotions. However, if a teacher lacks enthusiasm or genuine interest, then students are more inclined to disengage.

Teachers have a responsibility to cultivate a welcoming classroom culture that is accepting of mistakes. When teachers blame students for not understanding a concept, they create a hostile classroom environment where mistakes are not tolerated. This tension increases student stress and anxiety, creating conditions that are not conducive to inquiry and learning. Instead, when teachers normalize mistakes as a natural part of the problem-solving process, they give their students the freedom to explore and grapple with the math content. In such an environment, students feel comfortable taking chances because they are not afraid of being wrong.

Students need teachers that can help when they're having problems understanding difficult concepts. In doing so, educators may need to change how they teach the content. Since different people have unique learning styles, it's the job of the teacher to adapt to the needs of each student. Additionally, teachers should encourage students to explore alternate problem-solving strategies, even if it's not the preferred method of the educator.

FEAR OF BEING WRONG

Embarrassing situations can be traumatic, especially for young children and adolescents. These experiences can stay with people through their adult lives. Those with math anxiety may experience a fear of being wrong, especially in front of a group of peers. This fear can be paralyzing, interfering with the student's concentration and ability to focus on the problem at hand.

TIMED ASSESSMENTS

Timed assessments can help improve math fluency, but they often create unnecessary pressure for students to complete an unrealistic number of problems within a specified timeframe. Many studies have shown that timed assessments often result in increased levels of anxiety, reducing a student's overall competence and ability to problem-solve.

Debunking Math Myths

There are lots of myths about math that are related to the causes and development of math-related anxiety. Although these myths have been proven to be false, many people take them as fact. Let's go over a few of the most common myths about learning math.

MYTH: MEN ARE BETTER AT MATH THAN WOMEN

Math has a reputation for being a male-dominant subject, but this doesn't mean that men are inherently better at math than women. Many famous mathematical discoveries have been made by women. Katherine Johnson, Dame Mary Lucy Cartwright, and Marjorie Lee Brown are just a few of the many famous women mathematicians. Expecting to be good or bad at math because of your gender sets you up for stress and confusion. Math is a skill that can be learned, just like cooking or riding a bike.

MYTH: THERE IS ONLY ONE GOOD WAY TO SOLVE MATH PROBLEMS

There are many ways to get the correct answer when it comes to math. No two people have the same brain, so everyone takes a slightly different approach to problem-solving. Moreover, there isn't one way of problem-solving that's superior to another. Your way of working through a problem might differ from someone else's, and that is okay. Math can be a highly individualized process, so the best method for you should be the one that makes you feel the most comfortable and makes the most sense to you.

MYTH: MATH REQUIRES A GOOD MEMORY

For many years, mathematics was taught through memorization. However, learning in such a way hinders the development of critical thinking and conceptual understanding. These skill sets are much more valuable than basic memorization. For instance, you might be great at memorizing mathematical formulas, but if you don't understand what they mean, then you can't apply them to different scenarios in the real world. When a student is working from memory, they are limited in the strategies available to them to problem-solve. In other words, they assume there is only one correct way to do the math, which is the method they memorized. Having a variety of problem-solving options can help students figure out which method works best for them. Additionally, it provides students with a better understanding of how and why certain mathematical strategies work. While memorization can be helpful in some instances, it is not an absolute requirement for mathematicians.

MYTH: MATH IS NOT CREATIVE

Math requires imagination and intuition. Contrary to popular belief, it is a highly creative field. Mathematical creativity can help in developing new ways to think about and solve problems. Many people incorrectly assume that all things are either creative or analytical. However, this black-and-white view is limiting because the field of mathematics involves both creativity and logic.

MYTH: MATH ISN'T SUPPOSED TO BE FUN

Whoever told you that math isn't supposed to be fun is a liar. There are tons of math-based activities and games that foster friendly competition and engagement. Math is often best learned through play, and lots of mobile apps and computer games exemplify this.

Additionally, math can be an exceptionally collaborative and social experience. Studying or working through problems with a friend often makes the process a lot more fun. The excitement and satisfaction of solving a difficult problem with others is quite rewarding. Math can be fun if you look for ways to make it more collaborative and enjoyable.

MYTH: NOT EVERYONE IS CAPABLE OF LEARNING MATH

There's no such thing as a "math person." Although many people think that you're either good at math or you're not, this is simply not true. Everyone is capable of learning and applying mathematics. However, not everyone learns the same way. Since each person has a different learning style, the trick is to find the strategies and learning tools that work best for you. Some people learn best through hands-on experiences, and others find success through the use of visual aids. Others are auditory learners and learn best by hearing and listening. When people are overwhelmed or feel that math is too hard, it's often because they haven't found the learning strategy that works best for them.

MYTH: GOOD MATHEMATICIANS WORK QUICKLY AND NEVER MAKE MISTAKES

There is no prize for finishing first in math. It's not a race, and speed isn't a measure of your ability. Good mathematicians take their time to ensure their work is accurate. As you gain more experience and practice, you will naturally become faster and more confident.

Additionally, everyone makes mistakes, including good mathematicians. Mistakes are a normal part of the problem-solving process, and they're not a bad thing. The important thing is that we take the time to learn from our mistakes, understand where our misconceptions are, and move forward.

MYTH: YOU DON'T NEED MATH IN THE REAL WORLD

Our day-to-day lives are so infused with mathematical concepts that we often don't even realize when we're using math in the real world. In fact, most people tend to underestimate how much we do math in our everyday lives. It's involved in an enormous variety of daily activities such as shopping, baking, finances, and gardening, as well as in many careers, including architecture, nursing, design, and sales.

Tips and Strategies for Overcoming Math Anxiety

If your anxiety is getting in the way of your level of mathematical engagement, then there are lots of steps you can take. Check out the strategies below to start building confidence in math today.

Focus on Understanding, Not Memorization

Don't drive yourself crazy trying to memorize every single formula or mathematical process. Instead, shift your attention to understanding concepts. Those who prioritize memorization over conceptual understanding tend to have lower achievement levels in math. Students who memorize may be able to complete some math, but they don't understand the process well enough to apply it to different situations. Memorization comes with time and practice, but it won't help alleviate math anxiety. On the other hand, conceptual understanding will give you the building blocks of knowledge you need to build up your confidence.

Replace Negative Self-Talk with Positive Self-Talk

Start to notice how you think about yourself. Whenever you catch yourself thinking something negative, try replacing that thought with a positive affirmation. Instead of continuing the negative thought, pause to reframe the situation. For ideas on how to get started, take a look at the table below:

Instead of thinking...	Try thinking...
"I can't do this math." "I'm not a math person."	"I'm up for the challenge, and I'm training my brain in math."
"This problem is too hard."	"This problem is hard, so this might take some time and effort. I know I can do this."
"I give up."	"What strategies can help me solve this problem?"
"I made a mistake, so I'm not good at this."	"Everyone makes mistakes. Mistakes help me to grow and understand."
"I'll never be smart enough."	"I can figure this out, and I am smart enough."

Practice Mindfulness

Practicing mindfulness and focusing on your breathing can help alleviate some of the physical symptoms of math anxiety. By taking deep breaths, you can remind your nervous system that you are not in immediate danger. Doing so will reduce your heart rate and help with any irregular breathing or shakiness. Taking the edge off of the physiological effects of anxiety will clear your mind, allowing your brain to focus its energy on problem-solving.

Do Some Math Every Day

Think about learning math as if you were learning a foreign language. If you don't use it, you lose it. If you don't practice your math skills regularly, you'll have a harder time achieving comprehension and fluency. Set some amount of time aside each day, even if it's just for a few minutes, to practice. It might take some discipline to build a habit around this, but doing so will help increase your mathematical self-assurance.

Use All of Your Resources

Everyone has a different learning style, and there are plenty of resources out there to support all learners. When you get stuck on a math problem, think about the tools you have access to, and use them when applicable. Such resources may include flashcards, graphic organizers, study guides, interactive notebooks, and peer study groups. All of these are great tools to accommodate your individual learning style. Finding the tools and resources that work for your learning style will give you the confidence you need to succeed.

Realize That You Aren't Alone

Remind yourself that lots of other people struggle with math anxiety, including teachers, nurses, and even successful mathematicians. You aren't the only one who panics when faced with a new or challenging problem. It's probably much more common than you think. Realizing that you aren't alone in your experience can help put some distance between yourself and the emotions you feel about math. It also helps to normalize the anxiety and shift your perspective.

Ask Questions

If there's a concept you don't understand and you've tried everything you can, then it's okay to ask for help! You can always ask your teacher or professor for help. If you're not learning math in a traditional classroom, you may want to join a study group, work with a tutor, or talk to your friends. More often than not, you aren't the only one of your peers who needs clarity on a mathematical concept. Seeking understanding is a great way to increase self-confidence in math.

Remember That There's More Than One Way To Solve a Problem

Since everyone learns differently, it's best to focus on understanding a math problem with an approach that makes sense to you. If the way it's being taught is confusing to you, don't give up. Instead, work to understand the problem using a different technique. There's almost always more than one problem-solving method when it comes to math. Don't get stressed if one of them doesn't make sense to you. Instead, shift your focus to what does make sense. Chances are high that you know more than you think you do.

Visualization

Visualization is the process of creating images in your mind's eye. Picture yourself as a successful, confident mathematician. Think about how you would feel and how you would behave. What would your work area look like? How would you organize your belongings? The more you focus on something, the more likely you are to achieve it. Visualizing teaches your brain that you can achieve whatever it is that you want. Thinking about success in mathematics will lead to acting like a successful mathematician. This, in turn, leads to actual success.

Focus on the Easiest Problems First

To increase your confidence when working on a math test or assignment, try solving the easiest problems first. Doing so will remind you that you are successful in math and that you do have what it takes. This process will increase your belief in yourself, giving you the confidence you need to tackle more complex problems.

Find a Support Group

A study buddy, tutor, or peer group can go a long way in decreasing math-related anxiety. Such support systems offer lots of benefits, including a safe place to ask questions, additional practice with mathematical concepts, and an understanding of other problem-solving explanations that may work better for you. Equipping yourself with a support group is one of the fastest ways to eliminate math anxiety.

Reward Yourself for Working Hard

Recognize the amount of effort you're putting in to overcome your math anxiety. It's not an easy task, so you deserve acknowledgement. Surround yourself with people who will provide you with the positive reinforcement you deserve.

Remember, You Can Do This!

Conquering a fear of math can be challenging, but there are lots of strategies that can help you out. Your own beliefs about your mathematical capabilities can limit your potential. Working toward a growth mindset can have a tremendous impact on decreasing math-related anxiety and building confidence. By knowing the symptoms of math anxiety and recognizing common misconceptions about learning math, you can develop a plan to address your fear of math. Utilizing the strategies discussed can help you overcome this anxiety and build the confidence you need to succeed.

Online Resources

Due to our efforts to try to keep this book to a manageable length, we've created a link that will give you access to all of your online resources:

mometrix.com/resources719/terranextg4math

It's Your Moment, Let's Celebrate It!

Share your story @mometrixtestpreparation